Thomas Rumbold

An Answer to the Charges Exhibited against Sir Thomas Rumbold...

Thomas Rumbold

An Answer to the Charges Exhibited against Sir Thomas Rumbold...

ISBN/EAN: 9783744756716

Printed in Europe, USA, Canada, Australia, Japan

Cover: Foto ©Suzi / pixelio.de

More available books at **www.hansebooks.com**

AN ANSWER TO THE CHARGES

EXHIBITED AGAINST

Sir THOMAS RUMBOLD,

IN THE

REPORTS OF THE SECRET COMMITTEE

OF THE

HOUSE OF COMMONS,

AND IN THE

GENERAL LETTER

FROM THE

COURT OF DIRECTORS

Of the 10th of JANUARY, 1781.

By HIMSELF.

THE Severity, with which my Administration of the Government of Fort St. George has been arraigned by the Court of Directors, and by the Secret Committee of the House of Commons, may appear to have demanded from me an earlier Vindication of my Conduct. I am perfectly aware of the Prejudice, which their Proceedings, supported by a great deal of active though unavowed Calumny, must have created in the Opinion of the Public against me. I am not insensible of the Danger that may threaten my Fortune, and I feel most acutely the Wounds that have been given to my Reputation.——I well know what Sort of Spirit has dictated those Proceedings on one Part, and to what Object they are directed.——Yet, in the Face of such Attacks, as certainly called for Refutation, and might have provoked Resentment, I have hitherto observed a profound Silence. With some Men, this Forbearance may lead to a Presumption

tion that I am careless of my Character; with others, that I have nothing to urge in my Defence. The Time is now come, at which a Defence ought to appear. The following State of Facts will shew that it has not been improperly or unnecessarily deferred; and that, if my present Answer does not yet apply to *all* the Points, on which I have been publickly arraigned, it ought not to be imputed to any Reserve of mine, or to a Distrust in the Strength of any Part of my Cause. Let me only claim it of the Justice of my Country, to listen to my Defence with the same Attention, which has been given to the Accusations against me.—The Question is too serious to be decided by Assertions on either Side. I shall not follow the Example of those who have accused me. I will neither insinuate without asserting, nor assert without Proof.

The Court of Directors were in Possession of my Letter of *Resignation*, and had Reason to expect my immediate Arrival in England, when they *dismissed* me from a Service, which I had already *relinquished*. No Purpose of political Expediency or Necessity could be urged to justify this Proceeding. I no longer possessed the Powers, which I was said to have abused, and of which it might otherwise be necessary to disarm me by an instant Dismission. If the Court of Directors considered themselves as my *Judges*, they ought to have observed the Forms that belong to every judicial Act, which has Justice for its Object. They ought not to have proceeded to Condemnation and Punishment, (as far as Punishment was in their Reach) without hearing the Party. In my Case, no Purpose could be answered by it, but that of fixing a Stigma on my Character. The *Resolution* to dismiss me passed on the 14th December 1780. On the 20th, the

Chairman

INTRODUCTION. v

Chairman acquainted the Court of Proprietors that the Directors had appointed Lord Macartney to fucceed me, and the Appointment was confirmed as a Succeffion to a *Refignation*. My Letter was before the General Court, and two Courts were exprefsly held to confider of a Succeffor; yet the Proprietors were not informed that I was *difmiffed* from the Company's Service, or that there exifted any Caufe of Complaint againft me. This cannot be deemed an accidental or unintended Omiffion; nor can it be accounted for but by fuppofing that the Court of Directors knew that I had Friends among the Proprietors, who would have infifted on canvaffing the Merits of the Meafure, and who might have engaged a general Court to give it a fair Confideration.——I landed in Ireland on the 7th of January 1781, and wrote immediately to the Chairman to inform him of my Arrival. He muft have received my Letter on the 20th. The Bill in Chancery was filed againft me on the 29th, four Days before I arrived in London. Before it was filed, I might have been called upon to anfwer the Charges on which it was founded, or to explain fuch Parts of my Conduct as might be thought to require Explanation. No Point, of any effential Moment to the Company's Intereft, could have been gained by hurrying the Profecution in my Abfence, or loft by deferring it. With fair and impartial Men, I truft I fhall not fuffer from the Precipitation, if not Paffion, which has marked every Act and Refolution of the Court of Directors againft me, while they were the *fole Judges* of my Conduct. They are *Parties* now, and in that Character proceed with the fame Temper, and are governed by the fame Principles. On the 10th of January 1781, they figned their Letter of Difmiffion, purfuant to their Refolution of the 14th of December. On the Eleventh, they fent the following Inftructions to the Prefidency of Fort St. George.

b   Extract

INTRODUCTION.

Extract of the Company's General Letter to Fort St. George, 11th of January 1781, Para. 35.

" We hereby direct That you strictly enquire whether, in order to obtain their Leases, or Agreements, any Gratuity or Present hath been made, or given, directly or indirectly, by any Renter, Rajah, Zemindar, or other Person or Persons, to any Person whatever in the Service of the Company, and more especially to *any Member, or Members of our Council at Fort St. George,* and that you cause these our Orders to be notified to all and every such Person or Persons assuring them at the same Time, that upon giving Information thereof, and establishing the Facts by sufficient Proofs to enable us to recover the Money from our delinquent Servants, *the said Informants,* in settling their Accounts with the Company, *shall be allowed the Amount of every such Gift, Present, Gratuity, or Payment,* or so much thereof, for which they shall not have reaped proportionable Advantage; and we hereby authorize and direct you *to make such Allowances to them accordingly.*"

A higher Judgment than mine must determine how far the Spirit and Tendency of these Orders approach to Subornation. I shall only say that, with such powerful Encouragement and Protection to future Witnesses, it will not be extremely difficult for the Governing Power in the Carnatic to prove whatever the Court of Directors think proper.

INTRODUCTION.

The Bill in Chancery was succeeded by a Parliamentary Inquiry into my Conduct. A Man must be criminal indeed, whom it is not deemed unjust to prosecute in two Courts for the same Offences, at the same Instant. In other Cases, it may have happened, that the Discoveries, made in one Court, might lead to and justify more general or stricter Proceedings in another. In mine, a general Certainty of Guilt seems previously to be taken for granted, and engages the two highest Jurisdictions of the State, at the same Moment, to look for the Proofs of it, wherever they can be found.

The most innocent Man that lives might be perplexed to acquit himself against two such Attacks at once; especially if he knew that his Accusers had the Management and Disposition of the greatest Part of the Evidence in one Quarter where he had never been heard; and that he could not defend himself against the Charges founded on that Evidence, without the Irregularity of anticipating the Defence demanded of him in another Court, nor without disrespect to the Magistrate, who presides in it.

Such has been my Situation. The Secret Committee, when they undertook their present Office, professed themselves to be ignorant of India Affairs. The Knowledge they now possess, has been obtained by Inquiries, directed to a particular Point. The Records of the India House, that relate to the Subject of those Inquiries, are voluminous to Excess. The Secret Committee I am satisfied, intended

INTRODUCTION.

tended to confult them fairly. But through this Labyrinth of Papers, they have had no Clue to conduct them, except the Candour of the *Court of Directors* whofe quality of *Parties* fhould have been deemed a valid Reafon for not trufting *them* exclufively with the Selection of the Evidence. Had I been called upon to anfwer for myfelf, or to explain any Part of my Conduct, as I naturally expected to be before a Report of it was made to the Houfe of Commons, I could have pointed out other Papers and Documents, which the Committee have not feen or confulted, though very material to many Queftions, on which they have pronounced.

The Subftance of the Reports, which have been yet publifhed, (as far as they affect or relate to that Part of my Conduct, of which I now offer a Vindication to the Public) is little more than a Repetition of the Letter from the Court of Directors, in which the Charges againft me are enumerated. The Commentaries upon it are taken from the fame Source.

The Notice given by the Chairman of the Secret Committee that he propofes, at an early Day, to move certain Refolutions in the Houfe, which muft of Neceffity be founded on the Reports already brought up, and therefore cannot but involve Queftions, in which I muft be effentially concerned, obliges me to break through the Forms which have hitherto withheld me from coming forward in my Defence.

I am ftill fenfible that there is fome Imprudence in furnifhing my Profecutors in a Court of Equity with a Knowledge of any Part of

my

my Defence, until it comes regularly before that Court. But my Situation obliges me to give them that Advantage.——The Obfervations, however, which are contained in the following Papers reach only to that Part of the Charge which has been *compleated* by the Secret Committee. As they proceed in their Inquiries, and as faſt as their Reports are *perfected*, my Anſwers ſhall attend them.

The Houſe of Commons and the Nation will grant me that Audience, which has been denied me by the Court of Directors, and which I have not yet been able to obtain from the Secret Committee.

The Whole of my DEFENCE will be comprised under the following HEADS.

CHAP. I. Of the not employing a Committee of Circuit, but calling up the Northern Zemindars to Madras, and there settling with them for their Tribute.

CHAP. II. Of the Renting the Jaghire Lands to the Nabob for the Space of three Years.

CHAP. III. Of the Treaty with Bazalet Jung, and renting the Guntoor Circar to the Nabob.

CHAP. IV. Of the Application to the Subah Nizam Ally Cawn for a Remission or Abatement of the Tribute paid by the Company for the Northern Circars.

CHAP. V. Of the Prospect of an Invasion from Hyder Ally, with the State of the Troops, Fortifications, Finances, Stores, &c.

CHAPTER THE FIRST.

Of the not employing a Committee of Circuit; but calling up the Northern Zemindars to Madras, and there settling with them for their Tribute.

THE first Measure of my Administration, that attracts the Attention of the Committee of Secrecy, is, what they term *the Abolition of the Committee of Circuit.* " On the eighth " of February 1778," says the Report, " Sir Thomas Rumbold " arrived at Madras, and took upon him the Government; and in " about six Weeks after, he began the Abolition of this Committee.(a)"

It will soon appear that the Measure, referred to in this Outset of the Report, is stated with an Inaccuracy that may excite Surprise; but the Manner in which the same Measure is treated by *the Court of Directors,* must give rise to Sentiments of a very different Nature.

In the long Edict of Interdiction and Dismission dispatched from the India House on the 10th of January 1781 (b), *the Abolition of the Committee*

[a] See 2d Report, Page 7. (b) See Appendix, 2d Report, No. 153.

Committee of Circuit is attributed to the moſt corrupt Motives, and is alledged to be the chief Ground of the heavy Condemnation inflicted, by that Sentence, upon the Council of Madras. It takes the Lead of all other Offences, and is repreſented to have given Birth to them. It is at once the Apology of the honorable Directors for their own Ignorance of the eſſential Intereſts of the Company, and the Engine of their Vengeance againſt a Man, who, to ſpeak temperately, was better informed. They treat it as a Violation of their moſt poſitive and unequivocal Commands:—Commands that could not be miſtaken, and that gave no Latitude for the Exerciſe of Diſcretion (c). The Crime was wilful Diſobedience, and called for the ſevereſt Marks of their Reſentment. Accordingly, they diſmiſſed Me from the Service, without Reſerve; and involved two other Members of the Council in the ſame Sentence. Even Mr. Smith and Mr. Johnſon, in Spite of the avowed Merit of having oppoſed ſeveral Meaſures of my Adminiſtration, were excluded from their Seats in Council for having concurred in this obnoxious Point, "the "Abolition of the Committee of Circuit, which had been expreſsly "appointed by the Company (d)." The Laurels of Sir Hector Munro, could hardly afford him a Shelter from the general Proſcription (e).

I ſhall hope to be forgiven if I draw aſide the Reader's Attention, for a Moment, from the ſubject Matter of ſo much Indignation, and ſubmit to his Contemplation a ſimple Circumſtance, the Commentary to which will appear in the Progreſs of the enſuing Sheets.

The *principal Facts*, on which the foregoing Anathemas were founded, had *long* been in the Poſſeſſion of the honourable Court, before

---

(c) " The Court's Inſtructions were poſitive and unequivocal; they could not be miſtaken; no diſcretionary Power was given you to depart therefrom." See App. 2d Rep. No. 153. Par. 74.

(d) " The Conduct of Meſſrs. Smith and Johnſon, has, on ſome Occaſions, been commendable.—But as thoſe Gentlemen concurred in an Abolition of a Committee of Circuit, which had been expreſsly appointed by the Company, as that Act of Diſobedience of poſitive Orders has been ſo very prejudicial to our Intereſt, we can no longer deem Meſſrs. Smith and Johnſon to be fit Perſons to be of our Council, nor have any Share in the immediate Adminiſtration of our Government at Fort St. George." Ibid. Par. 161. Such was the Sentence of the Court of Directors on the 10th of January, 1781. In the Courſe of the *ſame* Month, theſe *ſame* Gentlemen were reſtored to the Councils Board, by the *ſame* Honourable Court, having the *ſame* Facts before them.

(e) Ibid. Par. the laſt.

before they ventured even to form an Opinion concerning their *Propriety* (*f*). The *whole Proceedings* relative to this obnoxious Measure reached them, at lateſt (we have their own Words for it) in January 1780 (*g*). The Letter of Diſmiſſion is dated in January 1781. By their own Account, their Reſentments were ſmothered for a twelvemonth. In faƈt, the Interval of Forbearance was far more conſiderable, and was marked by the thanks of the Company, and by a more honorable Diſtinƈtion moſt gracioufly conferred upon me by my Sovereign (*h*). The Thunder, however, gathered and broke in an Inſtant. Let them apologize for the Storm to thoſe upon whom it fell; or excuſe themſelves to their Conſtituents for the Calm that preceded: or let them ſubſcribe to what I ſhall hereafter offer as the Solution of both (*i*). I haſten to unfold to the Public the Heinouſneſs of the great Offence that is laid to my Charge.

The Provinces known by the Name of the five Northern Circars (undoubtedly one of the moſt important Acquiſitions that had ever been poſſeſſed by an European Power in Indoſtan) had been ten Years ceded

(*f*) "You were acquainted by our Letter, dated 16*th June*, 1779, that the *Propriety* of calling the Zemindars to the Preſidency, would be taken into Conſideration fo ſoon as your Proceedings were before us." Ibid. Par. the firſt. It is needleſs to obſerve, that the calling the Zemindars to the Preſidency, implies the Abolition of the Committee of Circuit. Both Circumſtances were announced in the ſame Diſpatches.

(*g*) "Your Revenue Confultations from the 14th March, to 17th Oƈtober, 1778, *per* Valentine, were not received till the 24th April laſt." (1780) "The Duplicates *per* Mount Stuart, arrived in January preceding; and we are ſorry to be obliged to acquaint you, that your Proceedings in that Department, have not our Approbation." (1781) Ibid. Par. 2d.

(*h*) It will be ſufficient to obſerve here, that when theſe Honors were conferred, and when my *Conduƈt* was declared by the Court of Directors, "*to have been very meritorious,*" the Meaſures which are *now* ſo violently attacked, were well known at the India Houſe. For the Proof of this, and for the particulars of the Thanks and Diſtinƈtions conferred, See my App. No. 1.

(*i*) As long ago as the End of the Year 1778, the Particulars of theſe crying, and ſelf-evident Offences, were known at the India Houſe—where they remained uncenſured until the Arrival of the Swallow Sloop, towards the Cloſe of the Year 1780. In that Ship the Governor General had ſent over a formal Remonſtrance, which I had tranſmitted to Bengal, on the Conduƈt and Principles *of the Maratta War*. Soon after, Diſpatches were received from myſelf, which made it ſtill more apparent, that my Concurrence was not to be expeƈted in the Meaſures purſuing at Bengal, and tending as I demonſtrated, and as the Event has fatally proved, to the Diſgrace and Ruin of the Company's Affairs. From that Moment the purſuit of my Deſtruƈtion, was conſidered as a Meaſure of fair Policy, by the Partizans of the Governor General. From that Moment, the very Meaſures of my Government, which had been approved both at Home, and at Bengal, were held out to the Public as inexpiable, and ſelf-evident Crimes! See my App. No. 1, and App. 2d Rep. No. 130, 131, 132, and 1ſt Rep. Page 41.

ceded to the Company, and overlooked by the Court of Directors, when it occurred to thofe faithful Adminiftrators, to appoint a *Committee of the Council at Fort St. George*, to make a Progrefs through the Country, in order to explore its Situation, and to afcertain its Refources. I fhall not here enter into the Merits of this favorite Inftitution. Let it be allowed to have been wife, politic, neceffary :-- It was fuddenly *abolifhed*; not by *me*; but by the Court of Directors.

The Orders for the Appointment of the Committee were carried out by Lord Pigot (*k*). They demand particular Attention, as they are the *only* Orders that have ever iffued from the Direction, with refpect to this important Bufinefs. They are, confequently, thofe exprefs, pofitive Orders, which could not be miftaken; which admitted of no difcretionary Interpretation; a Violation of which was to call forth all the Refentment of the honorable Court. The Orders, indeed, were not eafily to be miftaken. " We direct that a " Committee of *our Council*, confifting of *five* Members, be appointed " *to make the Circuit* of the Northern Circars (*l*)." It fhould be obferved that the Council under Lord Pigot had confifted of nineteen Members (*m*).

Let me now call the Attention of the Reader to the Form of the new Eftablifhment, in which I had the Honor to prefide. I anticipate his Aftonifhment! It was appointed to confift only of *fix* Members (including the Governor and the Commander in Chief) under ftrict Injunctions " *to remain at, and not be employed out of the Pre-* " *fidency* (*n*) *!*" I will not infult the Underftanding or the Feelings of the Public, by fuggefting a fingle Inference, or Reflection on this Occafion. But I cannot help remarking, that this Change in the Form of the Council is utterly unnoticed in the Report of the Secret

---

(*k*) In April 1775.
(*l*) See App. 2d Rep. No. 5. Par. 24.
(*m*) Ibid. No. 7.
(*n*) The Truth of this laft Affertion will be brought to light, whenever the Court of Directors fhall be compelled to produce Documents, to which they have refufed me Accefs, and which probably they have withheld from the Secret Committee, fince the Report afferts, " That this Commiffion was not ac- " companied with any collateral Inftructions." For the Number of the Members of Government, under the new Commiffion, See App. 2d Rep. No. 1.

Secret Committee, and that the Injunction to remain at the Presidency, is not to be discovered even in the Appendix.

Having thus acquitted myself of the Crime of *abolishing* a Committee which could not possible exist; of disobeying Orders, which the same honorable Court, from whence they issued, had forbidden, nay had rendered it impossible, to comply with:—Leaving to my honorable Employers the political Merit of having reduced the Condition of their Servants to a State of motionless Equipoise; establishing by one Regulation, counteracting by a second,—but without annulling the first, in order to reserve to themselves, in any Event, an Opportunity of Vengeance and merciless Persecution: Let us turn our Eyes to what has really been done, in the Midst of these Contradictions, by others, as well as myself.

The Troubles, that distracted the Government of Lord Pigot, prevented, under his Administration, the complete Execution of the Orders, which his Lordship had carried out. Under the Government which followed, a Committee of Circuit took place, but with a manifest Deviation, and in the most essential Point, from those positive Orders, from which it afterwards became so criminal to depart. This important Trust was committed to *two* Members of the Council, and *three junior Servants* (*o*). Under the Government, which immediately preceded mine, a Committee of Circuit was, indeed, appointed; but, in direct Contradiction both to the Letter and the Spirit of the Orders carried out by Lord Pigot, *it was entirely composed of junior Servants* (*p*). Yet the Secret Committee remark, " That the " two Governments which preceded that of Sir Thomas Rumbold, " *saw this Measure in the same Light with the Court of Directors.*" I believe that *one* of the Governments, here alluded to, little expected to be held out by the Secret Committee, as a Standard of Political Perfection, or the *other*, to be recommended as a Pattern of scrupulous Obedience.

(*o*) " We are under the Necessity of deviat-
" ing from the Orders of our Honourable
" Masters, with Respect to the Committee of
" Circuit." See App. 2d Rep. No. 7. The whole Number is curious, and deserves particular Attention.

(*p*) See App. 2d Rep. No. 11.

It may perhaps be said that thefe new Regulations were confidered as *Conftructions* of the original Orders. Be it fo. I fhall not condefcend to defend myfelf againft the Charge of having refufed to *conftrue* a Negative into an Affirmative. Nor will the Court of Directors, I fhould think, be very ready to admit this Idea of Conftructions, after all the Advantages they have derived from the oppofite Doctrine of rigid Conformity, of ftrict and literal Obedience. Something, it is true, they have hinted in the 92d Article of the Verbofa et grandis Epiftola, about Conftruction: But the Idea is dropped, after having furnifhed them an Opportunity of introducing a Contradiction in Terms; They talk of a *Conftruction* of *exprefs* Orders! They are evidently embarraffed, and inftantly renounce the Subject, to return to their favorite and fruitful Topic of *pofitive* Orders, that were to be obeyed without Modification or Difcuffion.

In my peculiar Situation, and in the midft of the Diftreffes that furrounded the Company's Affairs, when I affumed the Government, I was indeed compelled to have recourfe to a *Conftruction* of the Orders of the Honourable Court. The Spirit and Intention of the original Orders, by which the Committee of Circuit was appointed, was evidently, to introduce a direct Intercourfe between the diftant Dependencies, and the Prefidency; to deftroy too clofe and intimate a Connection between the Tributaries and Renters of the Company, and their junior Servants; to reform the Abufes, that had long difgraced the Subordinacies, and to reftore its Dignity and Controul to the Council at Fort St. George. But in what Manner was this great Object to be effected? The abfurd and contradictory Regulations of the honourable Court, had rendered it impoffible for the Council to move towards the Zemindars:—What then remained but to bring up the Zemindars to the Council? In the Dilemma, to which the honourable Court had reduced their Servants, it was the only practicable Meafure that prefented itfelf. And in the Conjuncture, in which it was adopted, it was perhaps the only politic Meafure that could have been devifed. It had the double Recommendation of being fummary in its Effect, at the fame Time that it refpected the ancient Habits and Prejudices of the Country in the Mode. Under the Mogul Domination, the dependent Princes were bound to pay Homage, as well as Tribute, once in every Year, at the Court of the Soubah. Thus, both the Dignity

and

and the Interests of the Company were consulted, in calling up the Zemindars to the Presidency.

That the first Suggestion of such a Measure should spread an instant Alarm, and excite a general Conspiracy among the subordinate Chiefs and Councils, was perhaps, the surest Test of its Utility. It struck directly at their Consequence, not to say their Craft. It was to reduce them from a State, little inferior to that of Sovereign Power, to their proper Condition of Collectors for the Presidency. During twelve Years, they had governed the Affairs of the Circars by their absolute Authority:—With what Advantage to the Company, is demonstrated, by the Amount of hopeless Balances, and by the general Ruin of the Zemindaries; with what Satisfaction to themselves, may be inferred from the universal Apprehension so clamorously expressed of the Interference of the Council.

That the Zemindars should be universally disinclined to concur in any Investigation that could tend to enhance their Tribute, or to expedite the Liquidation of Accounts which had, perhaps, been purposely embroiled, was not unnatural. They were influenced by a Spirit of inherent and irreconcilable Opposition (not dependent on any Regulations of the Council at Fort St. George, but founded in the eternal Nature of Things) between the Interests of those who pay, and those who receive.

That there should exist a striking Conformity in the Opinions, a friendly Sympathy in the Sentiments of the Company's Collectors and their Tributaries, may also, for ought I know, be sufficiently natural:—But I appeal to the Candour of the Secret Committee themselves, whether in common Cases, they would not regard such an Uniformity of Wishes between the Stewards and the Farmers of a distant and unproductive Property, as a suspicious Circumstance, and by no means favourable to the Principals.

The Truth is, the Natives and the Councils of the Subordinates, had one common Interest, and one common Object, the Suppression of all Enquiry. Their Sentiments, however, with Respect to the different *Modes* of Enquiry, were widely different: And in the present fent Occurrence, the former were in a great Measure stimulated to their Oppofition by the Intrigues of the Latter (*q*). The Former would naturally complain of every Regulation calculated to improve the Revenue in the Circars, as an Hardship ruinous to their Affairs. The jealoufy of the *Letter* was folely confined to the examining Eye of their Superiors. The institution of the Committee of Circuit had occafioned *them* but little Anxiety; partly, becaufe the Operations of fuch a Board were necefsarily flow (*r*); partly becaufe it was eafy to create perpetual Obstructions to its Progrefs; but principally, becaufe by an additional *Construction* of the Company's Orders, *they* were deemed capable of occupying a Place at that Board; and by that Means, with the Gratification of a new Appointment, they became Controllers of their own Defaults.

But let the Reader attend to the Consternation which overwhelmed the *Zemindars* upon the Appointment of this Committee;—This favourite Committee, the very Corruption of which was to be treated as facred,—thofe very Zemindars, whofe Favour was to be conciliated at whatever Expence, whom it was the moft inexpiable of Crimes to irritate or difguft! The Picture afks no colouring from my Hand; it is given in all its Strength by the Board of Circuit itfelf.

" The Appointment of the Committee of Circuit may naturally
" be fuppofed to have created very great Alarms among the Zemindars
" in general,—thofe who may have found Means to inform them-
" felves of the Company's Intentions, will endeavour to engage the
" other Zemindars in a Combination to *oppofe* their being carried into
" Execution—no more Dependence can be placed on their Attach-
" ment to our Intereft, now the Alarm is given, than if *Hoftilities*
" *had actually commenced againft them* (*s*).

I may furely, without Offence, be allowed to contraft this Scene of Terror and Diftruft with the " Reluctance" *faid* to have been fhewn by the Zemindars, to comply with the Meafure, which I am defending.

(*q*) Ibid. No. 30. to execute. See App. 2d Rep. No. 6.
(*r*) Lord Pigot maintained that the Bufinefs (*s*) Ibid. No. 18.
of the Committee of Circuit, would take Years

defending. What were the mighty Mischiefs refulting from it (*t*)? What the *Grounds* of this fuppofed univerfal Reluctance? Take them as they ftand recorded in the Report. "One Zemindar was idle; "one was poor; one was bufy; a fourth was fat(*u*).

The Reader, I am perfuaded, is by this Time prepared to hear without Surprize, that the Meafure I am defending was adopted by the Council at Fort St. George, *unanimoufly*: Although a Part of that Council has by no Means been diftinguifhed by it's Difpofition to acquiefce in Opinions, becaufe they were *mine*: And although a Majority of them, having antecedently concurred in the Appointment of a fpurious Committee of Circuit, had Prejudices of their own to overcome, before they could embrace the new Ideas I prefented to them. They embraced them, however; but not (as is infinuated by the Secret Committee, and is with lefs Delicacy infifted on by the Court of Directors) without all the Knowledge of the Subject that could be obtained from long Experience and careful Invefigation. Their Conviction arofe from their perfect Poffeffion of the Bufinefs before them.

They felt the general Diftrefs of the Revenue, and were fenfible, that the Stoppage of all Payment from the Circars in particular was occafioned by Abufes, which had long fubfifted at the Subordinacies.

D They

(*t*) It was indeed pretended that this Meafure would obftruct the Liquidation of Accounts, and diftrefs the fubordinate Treafuries. But it is notorious, that the greater Part of the Zemindars did not fet out for the Prefidency until the End of May; that all Balances ought to have been paid by the End of March; but that no Payments whatfoever had been made, or were likely to be made. The Diftreffes of the Subordinacies were relieved by the Prefidency, but were not enhanced by the Meafure in queftion. See my App. No. 2.

(*u*) " In this Letter feveral Petitions are in- " clofed, prefented by the principal Zemin- " dars, reprefenting their Inability to perform " the Journey, for want of Money, and many " other Reafons; and among others, one of " them makes this Apology, That he is fo " exceedingly fat, that he has been unable to " walk out of his Houfe for many Years."

See 2d Rep. Page 10.—See the whole of that, and the following Page, in which it is remarkable, that no Authority is cited, but that of the Subordinates. The Attendance of fuch Zemindars, as gave plaufible Reafons, was difpenfed with. There are Thirty-one Zemindars in the Diftrict of Mafulipatam, of whom *Seventeen* only came to the Prefidency. The Zemindars, of the Ganjam Diftrict, were excufed without Exception; and Vizicram Rauze alone attended from the Diftrict of Vizagapatam.—The Force, which feemed to be ufed, to bring this laft to the Prefidency, was in reality addreffed to the Subordinate Council, who had a clear Intereft in keeping him away, and whofe Intrigues had prevented him from coming at an earlier Period. Upon the receipt of *my Letter*, he fet out without the fmalleft Hefitation. See my App. No. 3, and App. 2 Rep. No. 16, 28, 45.

They saw the absolute Necessity of controuling the Proceedings of those inferior Councils; and, with a View to that important Object, some of them had formerly thought themselves justifiable in consenting to the Appointment of a Committee of Circuit, composed of Members whose subordinate Stations in the Service (by the express and positive Orders of the Company, as well as the Spirit of the Institution) should have precluded them from belonging to that Board. But the Face of Things was now changed. The Progress of a Committee of Circuit, at the best, and in its best Form, a hazardous Experiment, would *now* have been fatal. Undoubted Intelligence had been received of approaching Hostilities with France. A formidable Body of French under the Command of Monf. Lally, were actually stationed in the Guntoor Circar, ready to avail themselves of the first Appearance of Disaffection in those Parts. The March of the Detachment from Bengal against the Marattas had spread a general Alarm. Hyder was in Motion. Monf. de Bellecombe, who was arrived at Pondicherry with extraordinary Powers, had sent an Embassy to that Chief, and had demanded a Conference with him. In these Circumstances, the Appearance of a Committee of Circuit would have shaken the Dependency of the Circars. On the other Hand, had the Intrigues and the Influence of the Subordinates been suffered to continue, all Hope of a Revenue from those Countries, must have been given up for ever. The only Measure which seemed calculated to obviate the Mischiefs that threatened us on all Sides, was *to treat with the Zemindars at the Presidency* (w). It remains to shew, That the Manner of treating with those Chiefs, and *the Agreements* concluded with them, were as little liable to Objection, as *the Measure itself.*

The first Remark upon this Subject, prefers against me a direct Charge of having usurped the Province of the whole Council, by precluding all Investigation, and taking upon myself exclusively the Settlement of the Leases.

" The

(w) While the Zemindars remained at the Presidency, they were in fact Hostages for the Allegiance of the Circars to the Company, amidst the Dangers which threatened us on all Sides; nor did they return to their Districts until the Credit of our Arms was established, by the Reduction of Pondicherry.

" The different Zemindars," says the Report, " were never treated
" with, in regard to the Leases of their Lands by the Board collectively,
" nor in Consequence of any Investigation before them, but merely
" by the Governor in Person, whose Report was in every Instance
" held to be sufficient (*x*)."

It cannot be expected that the Secret Committee should in an Instant of Time, have been able to unravel such a Mass of Confusion, as the Rules of the Company's Service: Nor is it my Business to enter into a Defence of those Rules. To *state* the Rule, in the present Case, will be more than sufficient for my Justification, and will fully counteract the Effect of a Suggestion, which recurs in every Branch of the Enquiries, relative to this Subject. I repeat it, I disclaim all Intention here, or in other Instances, of arraigning the Candour of the Secret Committee: But, what will the Reader think of the Equity of the Court of Directors, in having suffered the Committee to remain uninformed of a Circumstance which could be no Secret to the lowest Clerk in the India-House? It was not merely the Custom of the Service; it was the express Duty of my Office, to investigate, to treat, to report, and to suggest Proposals to the Board. In all Transactions, similar to those in Question, the President is the immediate acting Man. It is a peculiar Obligation, arising from the Nature of his Commission. It is a Trust, which is, in an especial Manner, committed to *him*; and it would be a Breach of that Trust to surrender it into other Hands. I appeal, for the Truth of these Positions, to the Evidence of every Man, who has ever been employed in the Service of the Company. Let me now make my Appeal to the Justice of the Public. I beg Leave to submit to them, a simple Fact without a Comment. The Court of Directors, not contented with withholding so essential a Circumstance from the Knowledge of the Secret Committee, have not scrupled, themselves, to found the Charge of a black Crime, upon this Exercise of a known and indispensible Duty.

I have said that it was the peculiar Province of the President, to enquire, to report, and to offer Proposals to the Board. But I will

not

(*x*) See 2d Rep. Page 11, 12.

not do the Council the Injuſtice to inſinuate that the State of the Zemindaries was inveſtigated by me alone. The ſame Sources of Information were open to every Member of the Board. The Zemindars were under no Reſtraint, but had a free Communication with all, who were deſirous to confer with them; and were perſonally known to all the Members of the Board. I ſubmitted to Council the beſt Lights my Induſtry could collect; and if the Board acquieſced in the Reſults of my Enquiries, it was doubtleſs becauſe they were confirmed by their own.

With Regard to the ſecond Obſervation of the Secret Committee, under this Head, it will be ſufficient to quote it, in the very Words of the Report. " Your Committee find that the Chief and Council of " Vizagapatam repreſented by a Letter of the 17th January, 1778, " That the *Practice* had ever been to receive *Reports* of the Ability " and Character of *thoſe who propoſed for Leaſes, from the Chief and Coun-* " *cil,* and *that they had been much mortified by being* overlooked in this " Inſtance (*y*)." The Reader may call to mind, that he has already been apprized of the Effects of this *Practice*. He will be able to judge too of the *Weight* which ſhould be allowed to Repreſentations coming from Perſons, not only confeſſedly piqued and out of Humour, but hurt perhaps in a far more ſenſible Part than their Vanity. A few Obſervations upon the following Paſſage of a Letter from that Board cited by the Secret Committee, will ſhew in what Temper of Mind it was written.

" On the 10th of April," ſays the Report, " about a Month after
" Sir Thomas Rumbold's Arrival, *the Gentlemen of Vizagapatam,*
" acquainted the Preſidency, that Setteram Rauze's Manager would
" pay nothing till he had Orders from his Maſter at Madras; and
" alſo acquainted them, that they had undeniable Proof that 131,000
" Rupees in Money and Grain, had been ſent to Setteram Rauze, at
" Madras, and that Bills were negociating to the Amount of 70,000
" more, which together is a Sum equal to one Year's Rent to the
" Company. They repreſented the Tenants as cruelly oppreſſed to
" make

(*y*) Ibid. Page 12.

" make up this Sum, and *state the Reason of their making this Com-*
" *munication to be*, that some Part of his Arrears might be secured (z).

Upon this whole Passage I shall beg Leave to observe, That *whatever might have been the Reasons of their making this Communication*, every Allegation contained in it, was flatly contradicted by Setteram Rauze; That the Allegations were not supported by any Shadow of Proof from Vizagapatam; That, even if the Rajah had thought proper to dispose of the Produce of his District at the best and usual Market, such an Act of private Oeconomy could not well have been strained into a public Crime; That, upon my Application to him, in Consequence of the Directions of the Board, he promised to provide immediately for the Payment of his first Installment; and, That this Promise, *made on the 24th of April, was fulfilled on the 1st of May immediately ensuing* (a). This last Circumstance must have been overlooked by the Secret Committee; they would not otherwise have been led to affirm, a little lower, " That the same kind of Promise was
" accepted by the President in July, which had been made, but not
" observed, in April preceding (b).

I must here add, that this second Promise was observed as punctually as the First, and that before the End of October following, the Whole of Setteram Rauze's Balances, due to the Company, did not exceed the Amount of 57,000 Rupees (c).

Before I accompany the Committee into the next Field of their Animadversions, I must take the Liberty to offer a Remark on the Introductory Sentence which leads to the new Object of Discussion. " Setteram Rauze" says the Report, " *having*, as above stated, *obtained*
" *his Lease of the Havilly Lands for Ten Years*, your Committee
" find, That, *the* President, on the 20th of July, entered largely
" into the Affairs of the Chicacole District (d)." It is impossible that an ordinary Reader should not conceive *the President* alluded to in the second Clause of this Sentence, and who had immediately before been the Subject of Discourse, to be the very Person *who had just granted*

E *the*

(z) Ibid.
(a) Setteram Rauze's Account Current with the Company. See App. 2d Rep. No. 54— and the President's Report to the Board, No. 34.

(b) See 2d Rep. Page 12.
(c) See App. 2d Rep. No. 54.
(d) See 2d Rep. Page 12.

the Ten Years Leafe: A Tranfaction which is mentioned here and in other Places, with much Reprehenfion, but in a Manner that may miflead the Judgment, with Refpect to the Perfon upon whom the Cenfure is intended to fall. I beg Leave therefore to obferve, once for all, That this Tranfaction was finally fettled before my Arrival at the Prefidency. In Juftice, however, to others, I muft add, that although the Leafe was granted for fomewhat too long a Period, (as I obferved at the Board) (*e*) yet the Lands were undoubtedly lett for more than their Value; and Setteram Rauze will pay dearly (*f*) for having entered into an Engagement to which he was ftimulated by a Spirit of Jealoufy and Oppofition. The Propofal from Padnaub Rauze, upon which fo much Strefs feems to be laid, was not prefented until the Leafe was known to be figned, and was a Manœuvre of the Subordinate of Vizagapatam, folely calculated to diftrefs Government (*g*).

I fhall now attempt to reduce into a narrow Compafs, what is ftated largely in the Report, relative to my Sentiments and Conduct with Refpect to the Vizianagrum Diftrict and Family. It is there faid, " That my declared Object was an Increafe of Tribute from that " Zemindary. That, profeffing that Motive, I recommended it to " the Board to appoint Setteram Rauze Duan or Minifter to his *Elder* " *Brother* the Rajah, and that he was accordingly fo appointed. " That the Board next proceeded to force a Reconciliation between the " two Brothers. That Vizieram Rauze's Obftinacy, in refufing to be " reconciled to his Brother, is reprefented to him, at the Board, to be " the Reafon of Setteram Rauze's Nomination to the Office of Duan.
" That

(*e*) See App. 2d Rep. No. 44.
(*f*) Ibid. No 20.
(*g*) The Amount of Setteram Rauze's Rent in Ten Years, will be Twenty-four Lacks, 60,000 Rupees. The offer of Padnaub Rauze would in the fame Time produce Twenty-five Lacks of Rupees. The Difference is 40,000 Rupees upon the whole Term, *and not* 40,000 Rupees *a Year, amounting to Four Lacks on the whole Term,* as is pofitively afferted by the Secret Committee, in the 15th Page of the 2d Report. The Propofal of Padnaub Rauze was received at the Prefidency, a Month after the Bargain with Setteram Rauze was finally concluded; for the *Demonftration* of thefe Points, fee App. 2d Rep. No. 39, 40. It may not be improper to obferve in this Place, that although the Arrears of Setteram Rauze are ftated by the Secret Committee to amount to 180,530 Rupees, at the Time that he became Renter of the Havilly Lands, yet, in Truth, he owed nothing to the Company at that Time. He could not be in Arrears on Account of the Farm before he held it; and he held no other Lands under the Company. The Balances due from the Havilly Lands, and amounting to 64,530 Rupees, were Debts of Vizieram Rauze. See App. 2d Rep. No. 54.

" That the Court of Directors exprefs great Surprize at this injurious
" Treatment of Vizieram Rauze, and at the arbitrary and unwarrant-
" able Manner in which Setteram Rauze was put in Poffeffion of the
" Revenues of his *Elder Brother*. That at a fubfequent Confultation,
" Vizieram Rauze is fpoken of unfavourably by the Prefident, and that
" a Letter is written to Vizagapatam, accufing Jaggernaut Rauze of
" various Sorts of Malverfation. That, neverthelefs, the Gentle-
" men of Vizagapatam had acquainted the Prefidency that Jaggernaut
" had made the only Payment which had been received; *acknow-*
" *ledging, however, that the remaining Balance amounted to Six Lacks*
" *and a Half*. That on the 18th of Auguft, the Prefidency reported
" to the Select Committee, that a Reconciliation had actually taken
" Place between the two Brothers, and ftated that late Advices from
" Vizagapatam fhewed the good Effects of the Meafures which had
" been taken (*b*)."

To underftand as well as to confute, whatever Charges or Infinuations may appear to be conveyed in thefe Remarks, it will be neceffary to take a fhort View of the Hiftory and Circumftances of the Rajahs of Vizianagrum.

Vizieram and Setteram Rauze were Nephews of Chunderamah Widow of the late Vizieram Rauze, Rajah of Vizianagrum, for his fuperior Qualities, furnamed the Great. This Woman, by her Ability and Intrigues, raifed her Favourite Nephew, Vizieram Rauze, to the Rajahfhip. In this Appointment, the Right of Elderfhip, which the Court of Directors affect to treat as indefeafible, was utterly fet at nought; Setteram Rauze, notwithftanding the pofitive Affertions of that Court to the contrary, being the *Elder* by feveral Years: and he feems to have entertained the fame Senfe of a Title founded on that Claim, as is in the prefent Inftance, unadvifedly *profeffed* by the honourable Court. Setteram afferted his Pretenfions, and after various Struggles to defeat the Succeffion of his *younger Brother Vizieram Rauze*, was at laft prevailed upon, by the Addrefs of the Aunt, to give up the Conteft, and to content himfelf with being invefted with the Power of the Government, leaving to his *younger Brother* the Rank

(*b*) See 2d Rep. Pages 12, 13, 14.

Rank and State attendant on the Rajahſhip (*i*). After the Death of this Woman, the Diſtrict was again thrown into Convulſions by the ambitious Views of Jaggernaut Rauze, a *Servant* of the Family, but a Man of Intrigue, who, having wrought upon the weak Rajah to quarrel with his Brother (*k*), and being powerfully ſupported by the Subordinate of Vizagapatam, uſurped the Duanſhip.

To form an adequate Idea of the Confuſion which reigned in the Vizianagrum Diſtrict at this Period, it will be neceſſary to have Recourſe to Documents, which the Court of Directors have hitherto thought proper to withhold from the Public; and, apparently, from the Secret Committee itſelf: I mean the whole of the Proceedings of the Vizagapatam Factory during the Chiefſhip of Mr. Johnſon. The Scene of Cabal, not to ſay worſe, which is there exhibited, will afford the beſt Juſtification of the Meaſures I am defending; and will ſhew how lightly ſo unreſerved a Credit has been given, to the partial and intereſted Repreſentations of the Subordinates.

In the mean Time, it will be ſufficient for my immediate Purpoſe, to obſerve, that the flouriſhing Condition of the Vizianagrum Diſtrict, under the Adminiſtration of Setteram Rauze, is a Point uncontroverted even by the Court of Directors, when it ſerves their turn; and that the fatal Effects produced in the Country by the Diſſenſions between the Brothers, conſtitute an eſſential Part of the Evidence delivered at the Revenue Board at Fort St. George, by the Dubaſh of the Company (*l*).

I ſhall now flatter myſelf, that I ſtand acquitted in the Judgment of every impartial Reader, of the Charge of having invaded the juſt Rights of Vizieram Rauze, by reſtoring his *Elder* Brother to a Station, which ſtrictly ſpeaking, was the ſtipulated *Price* of his *Birthright:* and I am confident, that the having produced a Reconciliation between the Brothers, is a Meaſure that muſt meet with the Approbation of every Man acquainted with the native Character of the Indians,

(*i*) See my App. No. 4.
(*k*) The Rajah had naturally the greateſt Affection for his Brother. See my App. No. 5.
(*l*) See App. 2d Rep. No. 45.

dians, among whom an Interruption of the Revenue, is the inevitable Refult of internal Commotion.

I have only to add, that the *Payment* for which fo much Merit is attributed to Jaggernaut Rauze, amounted to no more than 5000 Rupees; barely the thirtieth Part of his Debt (*m*).

From this Opening of the Tranfactions with the Vizianagrum Family, the Report makes a Tranfition to the Diftricts of Mazulipatam. For the fake of Method however, I fhall beg Leave, for the prefent, to pafs over the 2d, 3d, and 4th Paragraphs of Page 14th, fecond Report, and proceed to the 5th Paragraph, where the Bufinefs of Chicacole is refumed. Paffing over too, the firft Articles of that Paragraph, which are more fully difcuffed farther on, I fhall immediately enter upon the Subject of the Letter from Vizieram Rauze, *faid* (*n*) to have been produced at the Revenue Board by the Prefident.

" It appears to your Committee, That a Letter from Vizieram
" Rauze, was produced by the Prefident at this Confultation, defir-
" ing to be reftored to his Fort ; and to have the Diftrict of Anca-
" pilly in Farm ; in which Letter he changed his Language as to
" Jaggernaut Rauze, reprefenting him at the Time of making his
" Requeft, in a different Light from what he had formerly done."

It will be fufficient to obferve curforily, that the Rajah's *Change of Language as to Jaggernaut Rauze*, the very Man who had fomented the Quarrel in his Family, can hardly be deemed extraordinary, after the Reconciliation had taken place. At any Rate, I cannot be held accountable for what is advanced by Vizieram Rauze upon that Subject, although I might fafely undertake to maintain the Truth of it. But I haften to the more important Charge, of having reftored the Rajah to the Palace of his Anceftors,—now magnified by the Court of Directors, for obvious Purpofes, into a *Fort* of dangerous Confequence.

(*m*) Ibid. No. 47, 54.
(*n*) This Letter, or Petition, was *not* produced by me. See App. 2d Rep. No. 51.

This *Fort* is described with equal Truth and Simplicity by the insulted Rajah himself. " My Fort is small," says he, " my House. " my Family, my Women are in it; they know this; it is not an " offenfive Fort; it is a common Eastern Defence round the Palace (*o*)."

The *Name* of a *Fort* was all that remained to the degraded Rajah of an Independency, which his Country had maintained from immemorial Time, through all the Succeffions of Tyranny which have overwhelmed the Provinces of Hindoftan. The Subordinate of Vizagapatam, more fatal to this unhappy Diftrict, than all the Scourges which had heretofore visited the East, did not scruple to obtain the Expulsion of this illustrious Chief from his *Manfion*, the poor Remains of his Dignity, his last Asylum from revolting Dependants, and the dearest Object of his Superftition (*p*). Oftentatious and fond of State, like all the Princes of the East, he groaned under the Indignity: fenfible of the Influence of Opinion, he trembled for the Fate of his Authority with the Inhabitants of the Country, and for the Security of his Revenue (*q*); oppressed with a Senfe of the Profanation that had been committed upon what he held most facred and inviolable, he abandoned himself to the deepest Affliction and Defpair. He encamped near the Pagoda of Sumachillum; and it was given out that he would not quit that Seat of Devotion, but continually employ himself in Supplication to his Deity, until he should be restored to his Fort.—Even the Board of Vizagapatam, although they treated his Piety with Scorn, and were probably little touched with his Distrefs, yet could not remain infenfible to the *Policy* of complying with his Intreaties (*r*). The Committee of Circuit had declared in August 1777, That " the Poffeffion of the Fort could not put it " in his Power to do Mifchief (*s*)." Subfequent to that Period, the Walls and Baftions had been almost demolished, and all the Military Stores and Ammunition removed (*t*). Lieutenant Eagle, an Officer of diftinguished Merit in the Company's Service, who had been appointed,

(*o*) See my App. No. 5. and fee App. 2d Rep. No. 20.
(*p*) Ibid. No. 5.
(*q*) See App. 2d Rep. No. 51.
(*r*) Ibid. No. 20, 23.—my App. No. 6.
(*s*) See App. 2d Rep. No. 18. Par. 21.

(*t*) Yet the Court of Directors are pleafed to remark emphatically, that the Prefidency ordered the Fort to be given up on the following *extraordinary* Condition: Namely, *That the Baftions and Walls fhall remain in their prefent Situation!* See App. 2d Rep. No. 153.

pointed, with the Rajah's Confent, to the Command of his Sibbendy, and to whom I applied for particular Information in this Occurrence, declared exprefsly, " That the Place was fo deftitute of " the Means of Defence, that it could only be confidered as a Place " of Safety to the Perfon of the Rajah, againft the Hill Polygars, " who frequently come down in great Numbers, and commit every " Sort of Depredation (*u*)."

In thefe Circumftances, if it was a Crime to reftore the Rajah to the crumbling Walls of his Palace, it was a Crime of which I muft abide the Confequences; for I am proud to avow the Part I took in the Tranfaction. The Council in this, as in moft other Points, were unanimous.

It will remain an eternal Reproach to the Company's Government in India, that it feems to have been a Principle of their Policy to drive every Native of Confequence out of their Territories. Let any Man, who has traced the Change from the happier Days of Bengal, and the Circars, to their prefent defolate and deferted State, come forward, and explain to the Nation, whofe Name and Honour are deeply concerned in the Queftion, what is become of that Train of Princes, Chiefs, and opulent Landholders, which once covered the Face of thofe Countries? It will appear, that they have either fled from, or funk under the Oppreffion of the Company's Government. I thank God, that I have left no fuch Stain upon my Adminiftration. But it is Time to return to the Report.

With regard to the fecond Petition, contained in the Letter from Vizieram Rauze, the Committee remark, " The Prefident *proceeded* " to obferve, that fince delivering in the former Petition, he had " obtained a verbal Agreement from Vizieram Rauze to pay 90,000 " Rupees for Ancapilly, which was immediately accepted by the " Board (*w*)."

Antecedent to my Adminiftration, the Zemindary in Queftion had been accepted in Mortgage by the Rajah, againft his Inclination, as a Security for a confiderable Advance made by him to the late Poffeffors,

(*u*) See my App. No. 6.   (*w*) See 2d Rep. Page 14.

sessors, for the Interest of the Company, under the Sanction of the Presidency, and at the pressing Instance of the Company's Servants. The Mortgagers having died without Issue, and the Amount of the Debt being about 10 Lacks of Rupees, the Rajah, in his Letter, had given the Alternative to the Presidency, either to pay off the Mortgage, which they had guaranteed, and to take Possession of the District, or to give up the Country to him, as a Part of his Zemindary. In the latter Case he had proposed to increase the old Jemmabundy from 65,000 to 80,000 Rupees a Year, and to pay an Annuity of 10,000 Rupees to the Relations of the late Zemindar. He afterwards agreed with me, verbally, to increase the *Tribute* to 90,000 Rupees a Year (*x*). This last Agreement was *verbal*, as is emphatically remarked in the Report; but it was ratified in the *Cowle* (*y*), which was wisely and unanimously granted to him by the Council.

The Committee proceed to state, "That the Adoption of Sette-
" ram's Son by Vizieram, (which he had notified at the same Time
" that he sent the Petition above-mentioned) was confirmed by the
" Board, and Setteram was accepted as Security for the Company's
" Tribute (*z*)."

The Practice of Adoption is not less frequent among the great Proprietors in Hindostan, than it was among the Romans, in the best and worst Periods of their Government; and is in Part founded on the same Principle. The Right is established in India, and until this Moment had been recognized by the Company. The Adoption in Question had taken Place before my Departure from England. No Attempt had been made to defeat its Effect, even during the Disputes between the Brothers. All Acts of Government had been carried on (by the Confession of Jaggernaut himself) in the Name of the adopted Nephew. It only remained for the Board to proceed with Circumspection, and without Prejudice to any lawful Claimant. The Adoption was accordingly admitted with all possible Precaution, and " so far as was consistent with the Rights, Privileges, and Cus-
" toms of the Country." With this Provision, it was resolved,
" That

(*x*) See App. 2d Rep. No. 51.   (*z*) See 2d Rep. Page 14.
(*y*) See the Records in the India House.

" That all Cowles be made out in future in the Name of Guzzi-
" petty Rauze." This Measure might eventually be beneficial, and could in no Case prove detrimental to the Company's Interests. But as it was expressly stipulated, that the Management of the Zemindary should continue in the Hands of Vizieram Rauze, it was thought prudent to make both him and his Brother answerable for the Tribute (*a*). In general, Security is only given for the Farms; it is never exacted from the Zemindars for their Jemmabundy. The Reason of this Difference is obvious; the Farms are the Property of the Company, while the Zemindars are the sole Proprietors of their Hereditary Lands. But all Distinction between those two Sources of Revenue, is every where confounded by the Court of Directors.

I come now to consider the Representation given in the Report, of the Agreement made under my Government for the Tribute of the Vizianagrum District. I shall state it, in all its Force, and shall then hope to draw the Reader's Attention to the real Circumstances and Grounds of the Agreement.

The Secret Committee in the Course of their Observations alledge,
" That the President declared the Jemmabundy of these Districts to
" be very inadequate; that he observed, that the Company would
" expect a Sum equal to the military Expences of which the Zemin-
" dar was now eased; that he stated that three Lacks, 5000 Rupees
" only, were paid to the Company, although seven Times that Sum
" was collected (*b*); That, however, he observed, at a subsequent
" Consultation, that he had found it difficult to bring the two
" Brothers to increase their *Rent* of three Lacks 5000 Rupees to
" four Lacks 5000 Rupees; that on another Occasion the Board
" agreed, that the President should once more endeavour to prevail
" on Vizieram to raise his Tribute. That on the 8th of October,
" the President reported his having endeavoured to prevail in this
" Point, but that Vizieram was inflexible; and that on the Presi-
" dent's Representation, a Lease for five Years was ordered, at four
" Lacks

(*a*) See App. 2d Rep. No. 44, 45. The Son's of Succession, evidently tended to secure their and the Family's Prosperity, was thus made Fidelity to the Company.
dependent on the good Management of the (*b*) See 2d Rep. Pages 12, 13.
Brothers; and this Confirmation of the Line

" Lacks 5000 Rupees. That the Enquiries which the Court of
" Directors enjoined before any Leafes fhould be made, were in no
" Degree attended to; and that the Regulations on Behalf of the
" Under Tenants, which they had prefcribed were equally difre-
" garded :—That the Committee of Circuit eftimated the total Value
" of the Produce of the Vizianagrum Zemindary at 20 Lacks : that
" this Account was more than confirmed by Setteram Rauze's De-
" claration to the Board; but that this very Witnefs to the increafed
" Value of thefe Lands, was himfelf made the Minifter over them, at
" the *Rent* of four Lacks 5000 Rupees (*c*)."

I fhall not lofe a Moment to obferve, that the Word *Rent* is not to be found in my Minutes upon this Occafion. From the Language which the Court of Directors have lately adopted, the Public muft be led to infer, that the Company have not barely fucceeded to certain Rights of Sovereignty in this Country, but that they are become exclufive Proprietors of the Soil! And that thefe noble Zemindars, the real and the fole Owners of the Lands, which they inherit from a Line of Anceftry that would appear fabulous in Europe, had on a fudden been converted into Farmers, or rather, Peafants and Labourers in the Company's Fields. The *Tribute*, not *Rent*, paid by thefe Chiefs to the Mogul Invaders (who were never able entirely to fubjugate their Country) was a Sort of Ranfom of their ancient Independence. It was the Price of a quiet Poffeffion of their Property, Priviledges, Cuftoms, and Habits. It was always affefled with Moderation; and with a juft Regard to the immenfe Eftablifhments, which the Opinion of the Country renders it neceffary for Perfons of their Confequence and Diftinction to keep on foot. The Soubah fettled with the Zemindars, without ever attempting to interfere with the Collection. It would have been happy for all Parties, if the fame wife Maxims had continued to be refpected after the Ceffion of the Circars to the Company. The Country would then have flourifhed, and the Company would have profpered in the Profperity of their Tributaries. To found this Profperity on the Bafis of reciprocal Confidence and Security, and to fix the Proportion of the Tribute on Principles of Policy and Juftice, were the ends of my

(*c*) Ibid. Page 15.

Inquiries, and the Objects of my Reprefentations to the Board, on this Subject. That the ruined Condition of the Zemindaries would not permit the Tribute to be advanced in the Proportions that I had expected and propofed, was to me a Source of inexpreffible Mortification. But I was compelled to yield to Circumftances. The Diftrefs of the Zemindars was great, and the Conjuncture critical. If the Prefidency had rejected the ultimate Propofal of the Rajahs, confenting to an Increafe of one Lack upon their Tribute, there would have remained no other Alternative, than to complete the Ruin begun by the Subordinates, and to fend Collectors into the Country (*d*). The general Difcontent and Confufion, which fuch a Meafure muft unavoidably have occafioned, might have given a fatal Turn to the important Operations at that Time carrying on to the Southward. The whole Force of the Carnatic, at that Period, was employed againft Pondicherry. The Refiftance of the Garrifon was obftinate, and the Succefs of the Siege began to be doubtful. The Treafury was empty. The Difputes between the Brothers, and the Mifconduct of the Subordinates, had nearly deprived us of all Revenue from the Chicacole Circar (*e*). The Draught of Troops from thofe Parts, occafioned by the Neceffities of the War, had left us but ill provided for rifquing the dangerous Meafure of feizing upon the Collections of the Country. In fuch Circumftances, I preferred a moderate but certain Increafe of the Revenue, to more brilliant but treacherous Hopes that led to hazardous Experiments. I fecured a Revenue. I did more; I fecured the Country. I knew that Conciliation was of as much Confequence as Tribute, and I confulted both, by extending the *Term* of the Agreement with the Zemindars. While a Manager of a Country labours under the conftant Apprehenfion of encreafing Exactions, the Cultivator is in an equal State of Uncertainty and Alarm. The Under-tenants, for whom the Court of Directors exprefs fo much affectionate Concern, will never engage with Spirit in the Bufinefs

---

(*d*) The Court of Directors, indeed, feem to advife this Meafure; for they make it a Reproach to the Prefidency, that they did not extort their own Terms, " from a Perfon " *entirely within their Power, and over whofe* " *Property they had* (as the Court *falfly* alledge, but with an evident Approbation of the Principle) " affumed and exercifed the " moft abfolute and unlimited Controul !" See App. 2d Rep. No. 153. Par. 55. I have been informed that in Bengal, the Court of Directors fpeak out, and fairly ftile the Zemindars the Company's *Collectors*.

(*e*) See Statement of Balances. App. 2d Rep. No. 54. The Revenue was abfolutely at a Stand.

ness of Cultivation, until they know whether any Part of their Crop is to remain to them. Men do not work for the Satisfaction of working. Security and Stability alone give Springs to Induſtry. The Agreement I entered into for the fixed Term of five Years, *may* perhaps enable the Country to recover from its languiſhing Condition. Such a Meaſure was at leaſt calculated to reſtore ſome Degree of Credit to the Company's Government. In Fact, it has quieted the Minds of Men, who, having much Reaſon to murmur, may be ſuppoſed to have had ſome Diſpoſition to revolt. The Meaſures of my Adminiſtration had more Connection with the late Tranſactions in the Carnatic, than my Friends have been willing to admit ; a Connection, of a Nature equally honorable to me, and beneficial to the Service. I eſtabliſhed Tranquillity in the Circars ; where, at the *preſent* Period, more than at any other, it is eſſential to the Preſervation of our Influence or Dominion over them, that no juſt Cauſe of Diſcontent, or Pretence for Complaint ſhould be furniſhed by Government. Hyder's Plan and Principles of Government ſtand high in the Eſtimation of the Inhabitants of thoſe Countries. If they had been irritated *at that Criſis*, by ſo offenſive an Innovation as the Progreſs of a Committee of Circuit, whether ſpurious or legitimate ; or if the Uncertainty of their Tenure, or the Vexations of Government had driven them to change ; they would have found a Protector in Hyder Ally, who by making an effectual Uſe of the numerous Advantages he would have derived from the Acquiſition of the Circars, might, at this Time, have been Maſter of the whole Coaſt of Coromandel, and might have accelerated the ruin of the Engliſh Affairs in Hindonſtan.

But to return to the ſpecific Points of the Charges I am at preſent conſidering. I was indeed little prepared to find the Zemindaries, and the Zemindars ſo totally ruined as an accurate and diligent Inveſtigation afterwards ſhewed them to be. My Calculation, however, of their Wealth, had never been ſo extravagant as that which is attributed to me in the Report ; nor does it appear from any of the References of the ſecond Report, that I ever made the Declaration there aſcribed to me, " That the Sum collected in the Vizianagrum " Diſtrict was ſeven Times more than the Sum paid to the Com-
" pany." A Declaration of a ſimilar Nature is with more Truth,

attributed

attributed to Setteram Rauze. His Evidence in this Inftance was, I fuppofe, exaggerated; or perhaps it was mifunderftood, and he meant to fpeak of the grofs Amount of the Revenue, without allowing for Deductions on Account of Collection, Sibbendy, and all the immenfe Expences of the Rajah's Eftablifhment. At any Rate I can have no Intereft in difputing the moft exaggerated Statement of the Profperity of the Country during his Miniftry. If by wife Management he in truth raifed the annual Revenue of the Diftrict at a former Period, from feven Lacks to twenty-two, he was the fitteft Perfon to fuperfede Jaggernaut, who, with the Support of the Factory at Vizagapatam, and by every Species of Malverfation, had defeated the good Effects of Setteram's firft Adminiftration, and brought the Country to the Brink of Deftruction (*f*).

It remains to fpeak of the Sibbendy, from the fuppofed Suppreffion of which, I had flattered myfelf with fo promifing an Expectation of an immenfe Acceffion to the Revenue. Unfortunately that Suppreffion was only *fuppofed*. I had been drawn into this mortifying Miftake, by the very Authority, which has fo often led the Secret Committee into Error, and which has furnifhed fuch ample Materials for Mifreprefentation to others, who were not forry to be mifled. The Reader will eafily conceive, that the Authority I allude to *is that* of the Gentlemen of Vizagapatam. That Board was the only Channel of Communication between the Circars and Fort St. George; an Abufe, the fatal Effects of which will long be felt in thofe devoted Countries; although a partial Reformation was attempted under my Adminiftration, by eftablifhing *Vackeels* (*g*) at the Prefidency. From the Reprefentations of the Chief and Council of that Factory, the fame Error prevailed univerfally at Madras, which has fince been greedily devoured by the Court of Directors, and which has found its Way into the fecond Report of the Secret Committee. It was generally underftood that the Vizianagrum Troops had been difbanded, and that the Defence of the Zemindary had devolved upon the Company's Forces. Upon a more accurate Enquiry it was too foon difcovered, not only that the Reprefentation was falfe, but that the fuppofed Reduction was impracticable. The Troops, which had really

(*f*) See App. 2d Rep. No. 20, 22, 45.   (*g*) See 2d Rep. Page 15.

really been disbanded, were the few in Garrison at the Fort. The Savings, arising from that Reduction, could not be considerable, and were probably more than balanced by the Inconveniences which flowed in upon the Rajah, in Consequence of his Admission of the Company's Troops. The great Body of his Sibbendy were still on foot, and were either employed for the Security of the Revenue, or fixed in Stations where the Company's Seapoys could not easily have been prevailed on to remain (*h*). Nor, indeed, at the Time of finally settling the Tribute, could any Forces be spared from the Service for such Purposes. On the Contrary, it had become necessary to call the greatest Part of the Troops from the Northward; and there remained no other Means of Defence for the Zemindary, than a numerous Sibbendy. Thus it appears, that the Foundation of those flattering Hopes was visionary; and the glittering Prospects, so feelingly described by the Court of Directors, have vanished, I fear, for ever.

I might here rest the Defence of my Conduct relative to the Vizianagrum Districts and Family, if the Public alone were concerned. But the Court of Directors are fertile in Sophistries, and as one is refuted, another, or the old one in a new Shape, is sure to present itself.

The Report goes on, " Your Committee find, that the great Ob-
" ject of the Board, in putting the Power into Setteram's Hands,
" was said to be the speedy Recovery of Balances; and it has appeared
" that he was nominated in July 1778, and yet in January 1779,
" his, and his Brother's Balances were no less than 557,999 Rupees,
" besides the Expence of an Expedition undertaken on his Account,
" by Colonel Braithwaite, and 103,030 Rupees, for which Jagger-
" naut was directed to account with Setteram (*i*)."

Although the principal Facts, referred to in the foregoing Remarks, may be, *literally*, true; yet the Court of Directors cannot *now* be ignorant that the *Insinuations* intended to be conveyed in them, are false.

I

(*h*) See App. 2d Rep. No. 51. Many Instances may be produced, to shew how greatly
our Troops have suffered, whenever they have
moved towards the Hill Countries.
(*i*) See 2d Rep. Page 16.

I defy the honourable Court to controvert the Authenticity of the following Letter, or to pretend Ignorance of the Facts contained in it. To have suffered the Secret Committee to remain in an Error, which they only had the direct Means of correcting, is the same Thing as wilfully to have milled them.

Extract of a Letter from Mr. John Davidson, to Sir Thomas Rumbold, Bart. dated Vizagapatam 5th March 1780.

" I should do the Rajah Injustice if I did not inform you, that he *has exerted himself exceedingly*, since his Return from Madras to the District, he having paid upwards of one Year's Revenue, with the last Addition of Jemmabundy, viz.

1779 April 29th, Rupees	- - -	118,333
June 30th,	- - - -	25,000
July 15th,	- - - -	88,869
November 21st,	- - - -	287,303
1780 February 15th,	- - - -	252,084
	Rupees	771,589

It is true, that Setteram Rauze was nominated to the Duanship in July 1778, but it is also true, that the Brothers did not return to their Districts until December following. It is not therefore wonderful, that no great Progress should have been made in this troublesome Business so early as in January 1779, barely the Space of a Month after their Arrival. It should not however be forgotten, that large Payments of Revenue were promised and *made* by Setteram, while he remained at the Presidency.

The Circumstances which gave Rise to the Article of 103,030 Rupees, for which Jaggernaut was directed to account with Setteram, are briefly, as follows. Jaggernaut, the favourite Minister of the Court of Directors, had continued in the Management of the Havelly Lands for some little Time, even after the Date of Setteram's Lease. He had collected to the Amount of the Sum in Question, and

and had, as ufual, diffipated the Money. Setteram was compelled to make good the Deficiency, and was left to recover from Jaggernaut as he could.

The Secret Committee proceed to obferve, "That at the Time when Setteram was appointed Duan, the Rent had not been fettled, but was referred to his future Confideration and Adjuftment (k)." It fhould be remembered, that Setteram had long been difpoffeffed of his Government; That he was not ignorant of the Demands for Arrears and Debts, by which the Rajah was affailed on all Sides:—that he was no Stranger to the Manner in which the Country had been difmembered, and to Jaggernaut's ill Management in all Points. It was furely not unnatural to take Time to examine the Rajah's remaining Refources before he agreed for the future Tribute. The proper Officers were ordered to attend him in this Inveftigation (l).

The Secret Committee conclude their Remarks on my Tranfactions with the Vizianagrum Family, by taking Notice of "The Difapprobation ftrongly expreffed by the Court of Directors of the Reftoration of Setteram Rauze, to a Degree of Power, *which he had been found to abufe and convert to the Company's Detriment*; and by citing a Paffage from a Letter from Mr. Cafamajor, in order *to throw a Light on the comparative Attachment of the two Brothers* to the Company's Interefts (m)."

I know not from what Information the honourable Court have learned that Setteram had ever abufed his Power to the Company's Detriment. It is true, that in the Reports of the Board of Vizagapatam, he is fometimes reprefented as a Prodigy of Iniquity: but it is equally true, that the fame Board, when it ferves their Purpofe, fpeak of him in the moft favourable Terms, and impute all the Mifchiefs, which had happened, to the interefted Defigns and dangerous Intrigues of Jaggernaut (n).

With

(k) Ibid.
(l) See App. 2d Rep. No. 45.
(m) See 2d Rep. Pages 16, 17.

(n) See the Company's Records relative to Vizagapatam.

With the Aid of all the Light which Mr. Casamajor's Letter affords, I cannot discover any Proof of the Charges preferred against Setteram Rauze. The Insinuation " of his keeping away during " the Revolt of the Company's Sepoys, in a Manner that had the " Appearance of premeditated Delay (*o*), was merely conjectural, and " proved to be groundless (*p*)." If any Letters were " written to the

---

(*o*) See 2d Rep. Pages 16, 17.

(*p*) For the Refutation of these Charges against Setteram Rauze, and for the best and most satisfactory Justification of my Measures, the Evidence of Facts, and Experience in their Favor, the Reader is referred to the following Letter, lately received by me from the very Mr. Casamajor, whose Opinion is in this Place cited against me:—Extract of a Letter from J. H. Casamajor, Esq; to Sir Thomas Rumbold, dated Vizagapatam, 20th Dec. 1780.
" As I have taken up this Ground, I beg
" Leave to exercise your Patience a little
" longer, by informing you of the Situation
" of public Matters in this Circar; and I am
" the more inclined to do so, because I con-
" ceive you will derive Satisfaction from the
" Relation, being connected with the Subject,
" as one of the principal Transactions of your
" Government. On my Arrival here, I found
" the Province loaded with an Arrear to the
" Company, amounting altogether to Four-
" teen Lacks of Rupees, of which upwards of
" Twelve Lacks were due from the Viziana-
" grum Family, for Jemmabundy, and Havil-
" ly Rents, &c. Setteram Rauze, on whom
" all depended, did not return from Madras
" until the 8th of October, when he arrived
" at the Capital. His Managers, in his Ab-
" sence, always wanted to refer Matters to
" their Master, to gain Time; thus circum-
" stanced, and the Responsibility with which
" I considered myself invested from my Sta-
" tion, induced me to adopt, without Reserve,
" the Resolution of interfering by a certain
" Day in the Collections on the Part of the
" Company, but before the fixed Period ar-
" rived, I found an Alteration produced,
" which rendered such a Step unnecessary—
" Money was paid in fast into the Treasury.—
" On Setteram Rauze's Arrival, I gave him
" to understand, what I conceived to be the

" Line he ought to adopt, with Regard to his
" Duties connected with his Government, and
" that I did not tell it as a Matter of Opinion
" only, but that it must be attended to with-
" out Reserve or Evasion.—He saw the
" Necessity of following my Advice; and this
" Conduct has enabled me to Discharge my
" public Trust, with some Degree of Satis-
" faction, and it has met with the Approba-
" tion of the Presidency. I have been able
" to remit from the Collections, to the Trea-
" sury of the Presidency, 120,000 Rupees.
" I have in Readiness, to send by the very first
" Opportunity, 200,000 Rupees more. I
" have already advanced for the Investment
" 160,000 Rupees, and the Issues made for
" general Disbursements, from my Arrival to
" this Period, amounts to Rupees 200,000.
" So except about Sixty Thousand Rupees,
" which I found in the Chest on my Ar-
" rival, the Remainder, amounting to Rupees
" 620,000, has been collected from the Time
" I took Charge of this Office; and I have the
" best Hope from the Arrangements made, to
" be able to send a further Supply of 250,000
" Rupees at least to the Presidency by May,
" exclusive of the Two Lacks ready for that
" Purpose, and the 120,000 Rupees actually
" forwarded; and by the 20th April next,
" there will arise Expences at this Place,
" which will amount to about 200,000 Rupees,
" for general Disbursements, Provisions for
" Madras, and some Advances to keep the
" Weavers from starving; all which I shall be
" able to discharge from the Collections; and
" this exists not in Idea only, the greater Part
" you will see has been accomplished, and I
" have almost a moral Certainty of fulfilling
" the Rest, if this District continues in Peace;
" and then I shall have the Satisfaction to re-
" flect, that from the Transactions of my first
" Years Residence here, you will have no

I Reason

" little Zemindars to stop the revolted Sepoys (*q*), it is obvious that, although they were written in the Name of the Rajah, they must have been dictated by his Minister.

My Respect for the Secret Committee, obliges me, before I conclude this Head, to take some Notice of the Examination of Colonel Mathews; an Officer, of whose military Qualifications, I long ago expressed my Opinion, by appointing him with the Brevet of Major, to an important Command in the Circars; but to whose Knowledge of Revenue, or Judgment with Respect to the civil Administration of the Company's Affairs, I confess as Governor of the Settlement, I should, in no Case have thought it proper to refer. The Truth is, this Officer either had acquired no Experience in these Points, or *ought* to have acquired none. The Orders of the Company are express on this Subject, and absolutely forbid the Interference of their military Servants, in Matters dependent on the civil Department. Colonel Mathews has in his own Person had some Experience of the Inconveniences which may arise from an Interference of this Kind. His voluminous Controversy with the Chief and Council of Mazulipatam, if it proves nothing else, may serve to shew the Impropriety of departing from a professional Line. In the present Instance, he candidly confesses, that his Information was collected, *as long ago as the Year* 1775, not by himself, but by nameless *Servants*, whom he sent into the Villages for that Purpose (*r*).

The

" Reason to reproach yourself, for having done me the Favour to interest yourself in my Appointment. I have besides, since my Arrival, dispatched 500 Bales, worth about 120,000 Rupees, and by the End of next Month 500 more will be sent to the Presidency, being mostly the Produce of the Money advanced in my Time. And it may not be improper to Remark, by Way of Conclusion, that for many Years past this Subordinate never made Remittances of Cash, on the Contrary, it received Supplies for it's Investment.—Setteram Rauze is on a good Footing with his Brother, but as he finds he has many Enemies, he intends to live at Vizagapatam with his Family during these Times of public Distress."

(*q*) See 2d Rep. Page 17.

(*r*) One Instance may serve to shew, that the Information obtained by Colonel Mathews was as inaccurate as might be expected from the Channel through which he received it.—He states the Value of the Country lately taken from Severam Rauze, Rajah of Curripaum, at a Lack of Rupees. See his Evidence, App. 2d Rep. No. 17.—Juggah Row, the Company's Dubash, who has been employed many Years in the Business of the Revenue in the Vizagapatam District, and who could not be mistaken, makes the Value amount to only half the Sum. See his Evidence, App. 2d Rep. No. 45.

The Reader muſt have obſerved, that in this Reply to a great Multiplicity of Remarks upon my Tranſactions with the Vizianagrum Family, which lie ſcattered in various Parts of the Report, I have taken the Liberty to claſs the Objections and Anſwers in a continued and uninterrupted Series; in order to preſerve that Perſpicuity, Method, and Connection, without which it will be in vain to look for diſtinct Ideas, fair Argument, or juſt Concluſions. I ſhall purſue the ſame Order in ſpeaking of the Diſtrict of Maſulipatam.

My Firſt Object, in treating with the Zemindars, was to obtain a full, accurate, and circumſtantial Account of their Condition, of their Incumbrances, and Reſources, and of the beſt poſſible Means of removing the one, and of improving the other. It was well known that the Balances due to the Company were enormous (s). A further Statement of Debts to Soucars and others, amounting to near ſix Lacks of Pagodas, had been tranſmitted by Mr. Sadlier, Chief of Mazulipatam; their own Accounts repreſented the Demands upon them to be ſtill more conſiderable (t). Cultivation was neglected, becauſe their Tenure was precarious. The Miſ-rule of the Subordinates had attained it's laſt Exceſs. The Exigency of the Situation called for ſome deciſive Remedy; Delay was Ruin;. and the ſlow Inquiry, recommended by the Court of Directors, equally uſeleſs and impracticable. The Circumſtances of the Caſe were clear and indiſputable. The ſingle Expedient, which Policy could ſuggeſt, or the Criſis of Affairs would admit, was adopted by the Preſidency. A fixed Tribute, for a fixed Period, was the only Means of reſtoring Induſtry, of removing from the Minds of Men, the Terror of encreaſing Exactions, of giving Subſtance and Stability to the Rights of the Company. The Practice of granting yearly Leaſes, was undoubtedly more favourable to the Views of intereſted Individuals, but would ſoon have proved equally deſtructive to the Tribute and

---

(s) For a Statement of Balances due. See my App. No. 7. The Court of Directors, in one Place, acknowledge that the great Object, the Payment of Balances, had not been impeded by the Meaſure in queſtion; and, with ſtrict Juſtice, fix the Blame of the Accumulation of Arrears, upon their favourite Subordinates, the ſole Witneſſes and Authorities, againſt the Wiſdom or Propriety of the Meaſure. "Your "Preſident's Remark," ſay they, "That the "Mode which you intended to adopt, had "not impeded the Payment of former Ba-"lances, was very proper; and the Chief "and Council were highly blameable for ſuf-"fering the Zemindars to fall ſo greatly in "Arrears." See App. 2d Rep. No. 153. Par. 64.—See alſo App. 2d Rep. No. 30.

(t) See my App. No. 7.

and the Tributaries. On the other Hand, a certain Agreement for five Years, has given Confidence to the Proprietor, and Spirit to the Cultivator, and secured an Increase of Twelve and a Half *per Cent.* to the Revenue (*u*). It is remarked by the Secret Committee, on more than one Occasion, and with some Appearance of Dissatisfaction, "That this Addition was on the old Moorish Rental (*w*)." It will therefore be necessary to observe, that in all Additions to the Revenue, it has been the general, if not the constant Practice to fix the Proportion of the Increase upon the *Assaul Jumma*, or the old Bargain with the Moguls. In a Country where Usages, as such, become sacred, it is surely Policy to conform to them. I did so in the present Instance. But it must not from hence be inferred, that this Increase of Twelve and a Half *per Cent.* upon the old Rental, is the only Increase which has taken Place since the Government of the Moguls. The unhappy Natives have been no Gainers by this Deference to their ancient Forms. The Sum Total of the Additions made to the Revenue, at different Times, since the Accession of the Company to the Circars, amounts to above 50 *per Cent.* (*x*) upon the old Establishment. An enormous Exaction! And far more oppressive to the Zemindars, than an equal Augmentation would have proved, under their Mahomedan Masters; inasmuch as the Perquisites of the Mogul Officers are comprised in the Estimate which is improperly called the *Moorish Rental*; whereas, under the later Agreements, as existing when I came to the Government, those Perquisites were not taken into the Account, nor were the Extortions of the Company's Servants subject to any better Controul than their own Discretion.

The Report proceeds to observe, " That the exhausted State of " the Company's Treasury, and unavoidable Increase of public Ex- " pence were urged by the Governor as Reasons for taking low " Rents. (*y*)" They were indeed urged as Reasons for taking a real and

(*u*) See App. 2d Rep. No. 49.—See my App. No. 7.
(*w*) See 2d Rep. Pages 14, 17.
(*x*) For Instance, the Rajah Jaggyputty Rauze Zemindar of Peddapore, paid under the Mogul Government, Pagodas 93,493. Under the Government of the Company, as settled during my Administration, Pagodas 139,656 : 31 : 40.

And to all the other Zemindars, excepting one, whose Territory would not admit of it, the Increase was in the same, or in a greater Proportion. See App. 2d Rep. No. 40.
(*y*) " The exhausted State of the Company's " Treasury, and unavoidable Increase of pub- " lic Expence, were urged by the Governor " as Reasons for taking low Rents." See 2d Rep.

and permanent Revenue, inſtead of nominal Increaſes, which no Induſtry could enable the Zemindars to make good; they were urged as Reaſons for reſcuing them, in that Moment of their own and the Company's Diſtreſs, from the yearly Rapacity of ſubordinate Exactors. They were urged as Reaſons for avoiding, at that Criſis of public Danger, all ſpeculative Projects, which might retard Balances, ſtop the Revenue, and diſturb the Tranquillity of the Country. It is admitted that I alſo urged, "*That due Care ſhould be taken to re-cover outſtanding Balances* (z);" It might have been added, had ſuch a Confeſſion been conſiſtent with the Views of the Court of Directors, "*That thoſe Balances were actually in a Courſe of Liquidation* (a)."

The Report proceeds, " Upon theſe Terms it appears to your
" Committee, that many Leaſes were let without any more accurate
" Enquiry into Circumſtances, which could point out where the
" Juſtice of the Cauſe lay, between the Renter and under Tenants
" on the one Hand, and the Company on the other. Of this alſo,
" your Committee find, that the Court of Directors in their Letter
" of the 10th January 1781, expreſs themſelves in Terms of the
" ſtrongeſt Diſapprobation (b)."

I muſt again obſerve, that the Zemindars cannot with Propriety be conſidered as Renters. They are hereditary Poſſeſſors of the Lands, liable only to a Tribute, which has been raiſed above 50 per Cent. ſince they have become ſubject to the Dominion of the Company. The Cowles provide for the Security of the under Tenants, and it is the proper Office of the Chiefs of the Subordinates, to ſee that the Conditions of the Cowles are complied with (c).

K   I ſhall

Rep. Page 17. The Reader will be ſurpriſed to learn, that the Opinion here referred to, is expreſſed by me in 'the following Terms :—
" If any *certain Mode* can be adopted, that
" may do Juſtice to the Rajahs, and at the
" ſame Time add to the Revenue of the Com-
" pany, I ſhall be happy to join in promoting
" it; but in our preſent Situation of an
" actual War, and exhauſted Treaſury, I am
" clearly of Opinion, that *a certain eſtabliſhed*
" *Revenue* is preferable to any *ſpeculative*
" *Schemes*, even if they ſhould in the End be
" productive of a larger Tribute; and which
" probably might be attempted, with greater
" Proſpect of Succeſs, when we have a cer-
" tainty of Tranquillity in the Country, and
" nothing to apprehend from the Views of the
" French." See App. 2d Rep. No. 50.
(z) See 2d Rep. Page 17.
(a) See Company's Records.—See my App. No. 8.
(b) See 2d Rep. Page 17.
(c) See the Records of the Company.

I shall not here enter anew into the Consideration of the Merits of a Committee of Circuit. Let the Records of the Company be fairly brought forward, and it will be manifest beyond all Possibility of Dispute, that I was diligent in the Pursuit of the Information that was necessary to guide the Determinations of the Board; and that I was as successful in my Enquiries, as the Situation of Affairs would admit. The real Blame to which the Proceedings of the Board on this Occasion are exposed, consists in their having exacted *any* Increase of Tribute from the Zemindars, at that Period of their Distress; a Distress that cannot surely be unknown to those who have so feelingly represented the extreme *Difficulty* with which most of those Chiefs, " provided for the Expence of a Journey of 300 " Miles," and with which some of them, both in this and in other Districts " were enabled to maintain their Families with common " Decency at Home (*d*)." The Balances already due, were in Truth, too heavy to admit of an additional Load. But, " Tribute" is the constant Cry of the Court of Directors, nor can any Measure engage their Support, that does not come recommended by some new Imposition upon the Tributary. It became prudent to consent to a little Harm, in the Hope of insuring a greater Good; in the Hope of obtaining the Sanction of the honourable Court to an Arrangement, which has been demonstrated to be equally beneficial to the Zemindar and the Company. If that Arrangement be suffered to subsist, if the Peace of the Circars be maintained, and if at length the Subordinates do their Duty (*e*), every fresh Dispatch from India must bring additional Confirmation of all that I have advanced. And the honourable Court will act a more candid Part, if, instead of persisting in the " impossible" Attempt, " to ascertain the Amount of " Damage to be sustained by the Company, in consequence of my

" Engagements

(*d*) See 2d Rep. Page 10.

(*e*) " We see the Necessity upon this Occa-
" sion, of a vigorous Exertion of the *Powers*
" *you have lodged with us*, in the strongest
" Point of View, being fully persuaded that
" if we should fail at this Time, in the Exe-
" cution of *your Orders*, the best Opportunity
" of accomplishing them will certainly be
" lost."—" If the Measures we mean to
" pursue, receive your Approbation and Sup-

" port, *the whole of what is due* at this Period,
" not only from these last mentioned Zemin
" dars, *but from all the Tributaries* of this
" District, will be obtained from them."—
These Passages being extracted from a Letter
of the Chief and Council of Mazulipatam,
will hardly be suspected of Partiality in my
Favour, nor can the Court of Directors de-
cently dispute their Authority. See my App.
No. 8.

" Engagements (*f*)," they will avail themfelves of the ample Means they are probably poffeffed of already, *to afcertain* the Advantages fecured to the Company, and the Mifchiefs averted, by the Meafures eftablifhed in the Courfe of my Adminiftration.

Before I enter upon a Defence of the Agreements made for the Havilly Lands, and the Farms dependent on Mazulipatam, it will be neceffary to revert to two Paffages in the 11th Page of the fecond Report. " Your Committee have ftated above that the Board at Mazu-
" lipatam, had, by Letter of the 23d May, apprifed the Prefidency
" that certain Zemindars had fet out ; and they find that this Letter
" was received at Madras on the 12th June, and that on the 15th,
" which was three Days afterwards, the Prefidency directed the Gen-
" tlemen at Mazulipatam to advertife for Propofals to rent the feveral
" Farms under their Management for five, eight, or ten Years, but
" that on the 3d July, they were informed from Mazulipatam, that
" no Propofals whatever had been received."

" It appears to your Committee, that the Court of Directors, in
" their general Letter to Madras, dated 10th January, 1781, ani-
" madvert upon this, and acquaint that Prefidency, that it does not
" appear to them, that any Propofals could be expected, as almoft
" all thofe whofe Situation enabled them to bid, were at that Time
" called down to the Prefidency."

Admitting the Truth of moft of the Facts referred to in thefe Extracts, I deny the Inference which the Court of Directors affect to draw from them; and I believe I fhall be able to demonftrate, that the honourable Court *muft know perfectly well,* that there was no Manner of Ground, for the *Animadverfion* they have hazarded on this Occafion. For firft, the honourable Court muft know perfectly well, that the Farms of Mafulipatam had no Manner of Relation with the Zemindars who were then called to the Prefidency. On the one Hand, the Dignity of their Station will not permit them to hold Farms; and on the other Hand, the Prefidency would hardly have trufted them to People already in Arrears fo confiderably, for their

tributary

(*f*) See 2d Rep. Page 17.

tributary Lands. Advertifements, however, for letting the Farms, were put up in the moft publick Manner, as the honourable Court muft know, at the Prefidency as well as at the Subordinates. So that thofe who came to Madras, thofe who ftaid behind, and every Individual under the Company's Government, had an equal Opportunity of bidding for the Farms (g). In the next Place, the honourable Court know perfectly well, that although the firft Orders for advertifing the Farms were iffued three Days after Notice had been received at the Prefidency, that the Zemindars were on their Way to Madras, yet the Farms *were not let* until eight Months after the Notification of their Return to their feveral Diftricts. The Farms were firft ordered to be advertifed on the 15th July, 1778. The Zemindars were known to be returned to their Diftricts in December of the fame Year. The Farms were let the 10th Auguft, 1779 (h).

The Secret Committee have not thought proper to enter minutely into the Detail of the Tranfactions relative to the letting the Farms and Havelly Lands belonging to this Diftrict. It will therefore be fufficient to give a general View of the Circumftances and Principles on which thofe Bargains were founded. Thefe Points feem to have been wilfully mifreprefented by the Court of Directors, who, in this, as in moft other Inftances, have mifled the Secret Committee. A Variety of Bidders, differing in Character, Ability, and Security, had prefented themfelves for different Parcels of the Farms. But it appeared, that the Sum total of all the higheft Offers of the various Competitors for particular Portions, exceeded only in the Sum of 1000 Pagodas, the fingle Offer of Lechma Narfimvaloo for the Whole (i). The Character, Property, and Security of this Man, were clear and unexceptionable. One folid Renter has an evident Advantage over a Number, although of equal Solidity; becaufe, when all the Farms are in a fingle Hand, the Produce of one Farm may compenfate for the Failure of another. But in the prefent Inftance, there was no Room for Hefitation, as feveral of the higheft Bidders were deftitute of Reputation, and had no other Means of procuring any Sort of Security, than by mortgaging the very Farm they were defirous to Rent (k). It is true, that Venkata Pontaloo had

(g) See App. 2d Rep. No. 36.
(h) Ibid. No. 55.
(i) Ibid. No. 55.—and Company's Records
(k) Ibid. No. 55.

had out-bid Narſimvaloo, in a Sum that called my Attention to his Offer (*l*). But he was diſappointed of the Security he propoſed, which, moreover, was not equal to the Object. Pontaloo was therefore rejected, and Narſimvaloo became the Renter of the Farms he bad for, at an Advance of 5000 Pagodas (*m*); and Loll Doſs, the moſt reſponſible of all the Soucars, is his Security. The Salt Farms were granted to Swammy Pilla (*n*), upon the ſame Ground of ſolid Security. In a Word, the Certainty of a Revenue, was the great Object I kept conſtantly in View. To have delivered up the Farms to Adventurers merely becauſe they offered largely, muſt have been Folly or Breach of Truſt. In Confirmation of what is here ſet forth, I beg Leave to refer the Reader to a Letter of Mr. Cotsford, a Gentleman ſent from Europe, to take upon him the Chiefſhip of Mazulipatam, and ſince appointed by the Company to ſucceed to the Government (*o*).

Extract of a Letter from Mr. Cotsford, to Sir Thomas Rumbold, dated Mazulipatam, 19th Auguſt 1779.

" I am glad the Buſineſs of the Farms is decided, and am per-
" fectly ſatisfied *with the Manner in which it is done*. The Syſtem of
" Management, ſo far as our preſent Experience can enable us to
" judge of it, appears to me to have been a loſing one. And in
" Speculation, appears to have been the worſt that could have been
" adopted. I was ſome Days ago, on the Point of writing to you,
" to apprize you of the Inconveniences that were to be appre-
" hended, from any further Delay in this Matter of the Farms; but
" hearing that it was purely the Conſequence of your ill State of Health,
" and that we might expect to hear of the Diſpoſal of the Farms, at
" leaſt in a few Days, I laid aſide the Intention as unneceſſary."

I ſhall now attend the Secret Committee in their Remarks upon the Tranſactions of the Preſidency relative to the Diſtricts dependent upon

L *Ganjam* :

(*l*) See 2d Rep. Page 17.
(*m*) See App. 2d Rep. No. 55.
(*n*) Ibid.
(*o*) In Juſtification of theſe Sentiments of Mr. Cotsford, and of my own Meaſures, ſee the

Statement of regular Annual Diminutions in the Rents of theſe Farms, and at the ſame Time of regularly growing Arrears. See App. 2d Rep. No. 49.

Ganjam: I say the Secret Committee, for I shall not think myself obliged to pursue the Observations of *the Court of Directors* through *forty* Articles which they have bestowed upon this Subject, and in which, without producing a single Proof, they have allowed themselves to make Use of Expressions of Bitterness and Invective, which the Decorum of public Bodies usually excludes from their Proceedings (*p*).

" Your Committee found," says the Report, " that the Ganjam Zemindars had been ordered down to Madras; and, among others, a Man named Ball Kistnah, the Company's Dubash and Interpreter, as he is stiled in the Order, some of the Zemindars having been themselves dispensed with on sending Representatives; but, as to Ball Kistnah, the Order was repeated on the 28th of July 1778, with a good deal of Warmth, threatening him with the Danger of incurring their highest Displeasure, and two Companies of Sepoys (*q*)."

In all the Circars similar Causes operated to a similar Destruction of the Revenue. They operated, however, with increasing Effect, in Proportion as the Sphere of their Activity was removed from the Center of Account and Controul. Accordingly, *Ganjam*, the most distant of the Company's Establishments in the Circars, was equally distinguished by the Enormity of its Balances, and the Delinquency of its Subordinate. In Consideration of the impoverished State of the Zemindars in this ruined District, and their great Distance from Madras, their personal Attendance at the Presidency was dispensed with. But Ball Kistnah (who was not a Zemindar, as the Report seems to imply) had not the slightest Excuse to plead: He was a Servant of the Company, subject to the Orders of Council, and liable to

---

(*p*) See App. 2d Rep. No. 153. Par. 116, and elsewhere.

(*q*) See 2d Rep. Page 18. I must here observe, that in the Authorities referred to in the Report, there is no Mention to be found of *two Companies* of Sepoys. In the Orders first issued on this Subject, dated 15th April, 1778, and repeated *without any Warmth* the 21st July following, there is no Mention *whatever* made of " Sepoys," or " of the Danger of incurring our *highest* Displeasure." On the 28th of February, *in the following Year*, after Ball Kistnah had lingered several Months on the Road, it was indeed determined, if he should persist in his Disobedience, to have him sent up under *a Guard* of Sepoys; but the Idea of employing *two Companies* on that Service, was never in Contemplation at the Presidency. See App. 2d Rep. No. 26, 37, 56.

to be called before them, whenever, and in what Manner foever their Difcretion fhould prefcribe.

The Report proceeds, " It appeared to your Committee, That " *the Gentlemen of Ganjam* had reprefented to the Prefidency, that " this very Man had, under Cover of another Name, been the real " Renter of the Ganjam Havelly Lands, which were in Arrear " 182,666 Rupees; and that for Vizianagur, he was in Arrear 60,350 " Rupees, which he had engaged to pay; and this appears to your " Committee, *to be acknowledged by the Board*, in a Letter to " Ganjam, 21ft May 1779 (*r*)."

I muft take the Liberty to declare, that no fuch Acknowledgment was ever made by the Board. The Point was neither admitted nor denied, but was exprefsly referred " to a thorough Inveftigation " upon the Spot, after the Return of the Party (*s*)." But the Queftion is in itfelf of the utmoft Indifference. For, whether Ball Kiftnah or another had been the ancient Renter, the former gave Security, in the actual Occurrence, for the gradual Payment of the Balances. In one Cafe, the Company were clear Gainers; in the other, an uncertain Debt was put into a regular Courfe of Liquidation.

The Committee proceed to obferve, that this Man made two Propofals for renting the entire Revenue of the Diftrict; and they take Notice, that in the firft Propofal, which was rejected, *the Sea and Land Cuftoms were included*; but they have not thought proper to remark, that in the fecond Propofal, upon which the Agreement was formed, *thofe Cuftoms were exprefsly excepted*, and of Courfe, remain to be carried to the Account of the actual Revenue (*t*).

It is next alledged, " That Mr. Perring, expreffing his Opinion " that Ball Kiftnah was the fitteft Perfon to be the Renter, *yet ac-* " *knowledges*

(*r*) See 2d Rep. Page 18.
(*s*) The following are the exprefs Words ufed by the Board on this Occafion:—" As Ball " Kiftnah is fo foon to return to Ganjam, it " will then be proper that you enter upon a " thorough Inveftigation of this Matter, and

" if it proves he is the real Renter, you will " be careful that he makes good his Balances " to the Company." See App. 2d Rep. No. 57.
(*t*) See App. 2d Rep. No. 58, 60.

" knowledges that he offers lefs than the Chief and Council had been able themfelves to collect (*u*)"

Mr. Perring, when the Merits of the *firſt Propoſal* were under Deliberation, afferted the Offer to be "lefs than what was collected, by the Chief and Council, *for ſome Years before the late Troubles in the Goomſoor Country* (*w*)," which laſt Words are omitted in the Report. It will be needlefs to remark, how eſſentially thofe Words affect the Senfe of Mr. Perring's Minute; or how utterly they overthrow the general Idea, which the Quotation as it ſtands in the Report is calculated to convey (*x*).

The Report proceeds, " Mr. Johnfon fhewed from Experience, it had beenſ found difadvantageous to let the whole to any one Renter (*y*)"

The Reader will naturally conceive, that Mr. Johnfon has eſtabliſhed this Opinion by a Chain of Reafoning, fupported by a Deduction of Facts. Let us recur to his Minute. "The *inſuperable Objections*, fays he, to a Renter for *this* whole Diſtrict, and the *numerous Examples I have ſeen* of their Inſufficiency, *convinces me*, that the moſt eligible Plan is what I have fuggeſted (*z*)." This, it muſt be allowed, is a compendious Method of *ſhewing from Experience!* If the Reader wiſhes to defcend into Particulars, if he calls for one only of thefe infuperable Objections, if he aſks for *one* only of the numerous Examples which Mr. Johnfon had *ſeen*; upon thefe Details, the Minute will not afford him the flighteſt Satisfaction. He will be the lefs furprized, however, at this modeſt Silence, when he is informed, That the *Example in Queſtion* is the only Example of letting the Zemindaries in Farm (*a*) which has occurred in the Annals of

---

(*u*) See 2d Rep. Page 18.
(*w*) See App. 2d Rep. No. 59.
(*x*) Indeed it is not eafy to difcover for what Purpofe this Objection of Mr. Perring is quoted at all—It being an Objection to a Nullity, to a Meafure which did *not* take Place. A carelefs Reader might be led to confider it as an Argument againſt the Meafure which was really agreed to, and to which Mr. Perring gave his hearty Concurrence; both becaufe the Terms were raifed, and for other Reafons fuggeſted in the Papers I produced to the Board. See App. 2d Rep. No. 60, 61.
(*y*) See 2d Rep. Page 18.
(*z*) See App. 2d Rep. No. 59.
(*a*) The Reafons for adopting this Meafure in the prefent Inſtance, are fully ſet forth in my Minutes. See App. 2d Rep. No. 60, 61.— See My App. No. 9.

of the Company's Government in the Circars! Such are the Grounds on which the Court of Directors presume they shall stand justified in the Face of the World, for the Attacks they have levelled against the Fortune and Honour of an Individual, whose Views for the public Service have alone rendered him obnoxious to their Persecution! I throw myself upon the Justice of my Country. I appeal to a Tribunal, where Insinuation will not be received as Fact, or Assertion as Evidence; and, where vague and rash Declamation, will not be suffered to pass under the Description of *shewing from Experience*.

Mr. Johnson avows in this Minute, " That he entertains *great* " *Doubts* of the prudent Conduct of the Rajah of Goomsoor (*b*)." And he gives it as his Opinion, " That the Havelly Lands ought to re- " main in Mr. Mansell's the Collector's Hands, who had done his " Duty in every Respect (*c*)." It will soon appear, that this last Opinion is not better founded than many others, which the Court of Directors have adopted upon the Authority of this Gentleman.

The next Allegation in the Report is, " That the Gentlemen of " Ganjam had stated their Receipts for the last five Years at five " Lacks and upwards (*d*)." The Statement here referred to, does not appear in the Appendix; nor is it worth looking for, as it is flatly contradicted by the Balances; which had increased to an enormous Amount, notwithstanding the Mode of military Execution to which those Gentlemen had frequently Recourse in forcing Collections; and notwithstanding the happy Talent they possessed, as will presently be seen, of accounting for Balances.

" Ball Kistnah" says the Report, (speaking of his second Proposal) " offered a regular annual Payment, amounting in *ten Years* to " 415,000 Rupees, and a regular Discharge of Balances to the " Amount of 40,000 *Pagodas per Annum* (*e*)."

M   There

(*b*) See App. 2d Rep. No. 59.
(*c*) Ibid. This Opinion of Mr. Johnson stands in direct Contradiction with the express Orders of the Company; who in their Letter of the 26th March, 1768, direct as follows:—" Should " the Circars continue in our Possession, it " must be observed as a general Rule, that no " European is to interfere in the Collections " of the Revenue."
(*d*) See 2d Rep. Page 18.
(*e*) Ibid.

There is in this Reprefentation a Complication of Errors, which cannot eafily be accounted for. The Fact referred to is fimply as follows. Upon Condition of receiving a Leafe for ten Years, Ball Kiftnah offered a regular *annual Payment* of 415,000 Rupees, and a regular Difcharge of Balances to the annual Amount of 40,000 Rupees.

" This laft Article," continues the Report, (alluding to the erroneous Statement above-mentioned, of an annual Payment of 40,000 *Pagodas* for Balances) " the Directors in their Letter 10th January, " 1781, ftate to have been, in Truth, a Favour to himfelf, as he had " been in Fact the Renter from whom thofe Balances were really due, " and were then payable to their full Amount (*f*)."

Here again there occurs a Miftake in the Report, which is inexplicable. Ball Kiftnah had been *reprefented* (but the Fact was by no Means proved) to be the real Renter of the Havelly Lands, from whence confiderable Balances were due, which the Board tied him down to difcharge by annual Payments of 20,000 Rupees. Admitting the Suppofition of his having been the real Renter, this Arrangement might in fome Senfe be confidered as a Favour to him. But the Sum of 40,000 Rupees (not Pagodas) which he had propofed to pay annually, was in Difcharge of Balances due, not from himfelf, but from the Zemindars; it was the Confideration paid by him for a ten Years Leafe of the whole Diftrict, then firft rented. It was an original Condition in a new Bargain, and by no Means an Arrangement intended to *favour* him, in the Payment of what he might already owe. In ten Years, he expected by good Management, to be enabled to difcharge the old Debts of the Zemindars, as well as the accruing Tribute; and without fuch a Settlement, all Hopes both of one and the other, would, I believe, have been worfe than precarious (*g*).

" Ball Kiftnah affirmed," fays the Report, " That five Lacks was " unreafonable (*h*)." In common Juftice it fhould have been added, that what Ball Kiftnah affirmed, Mr. Smith has demonftrated. In the very Minute which is cited by the Report, in order to fhew that Gentleman's

(*f*) Ibid.
(*g*) See App. 2d Rep. No. 60.
(*h*) See 2d Rep. Page 18.

tleman's Opinion, respecting the large Amount of the Revenue, he has himself accounted for the Growth of the Arrears, and asserts positively, " That the Tribute exacted from many of the Zemindars, " was higher than their Countries would bear (*i*)". The Estimate, therefore of the nominal Tribute, and the State of the effective Collection, must for ever be at Variance: The inevitable Result of which, is Deception to the Company, and Vexation and Ruin to the Tributary.

So far, then, are Mr. Smith's Calculations from remaining " uncontradicted," that they are contradicted by himself (*k*). I may boldly say, that, in my Minutes, his whole Reasoning upon this Subject had been confuted before it was presented to the Board. I will add, that if those Minutes had appeared deserving of more Attention, it would not have been stated in the Report, " That the " Presidency did not appear to take Pains to get proper Data to " proceed upon (*l*)."

How far the Honour of the Presidency may be concerned to remove the other Imputation, thrown upon them in this Part of the Report, of having generally " disregarded the Information afforded " by the subordinate Factories (*m*)," the Public is in a Situation to determine. The general Views, Conduct, and Interests of those inferior Councils, have been laid fairly before them.

In what Degree the Presidency may have merited the particular Reprehension inflicted on them, in the present Instance, by the Secret Committee, for neglecting " the strong Representations made by the " Gentlemen of Ganjam, against the Agreement with Ball Kistnah (*n*)," will appear from the following State of Facts.

In the Year 1778, (the Year immediately following the boasted Restoration of the Revenue, during the Chiefship of Mr. Smith) the whole Collections, including a Variety of old Balances, as well as what could be obtained of the current Tribute, fell short of the Amount

(*i*) See App. 2d Rep. No. 61.   (*m*) Ibid. Page 19.
(*k*) See my App. No. 9.   (*n*) Ibid.
(*l*) See 2d Rep. Page 18.

Amount of the simple yearly Revenue, as stated in the Report, by a Sum considerably exceeding One-third. In the following Year (1779) the whole Mass of these mixed Collections did not amount to one Half of the expected simple Revenue of the Year. So rapid a Decline of the Revenue did not fail to excite in my Mind a serious Alarm, not unmixed with Suspicion. It is true, the Collections of the current Year had only been continued to the End of February (*o*). But the Year's Account finishes in April; and the Collections of the two remaining Months could not possibly be considerable. In the mean Time, the Expences of the Establishment were absorbing the whole Produce of the Collections (*p*). I determined to attempt an immediate Reform. But,—upon the first Rumour of this Intention,—to the inexpressible Astonishment of every Member of the Council, without Exception,—the Gentlemen of Ganjam remitted an Account to the Presidency of a *pretended* Collection, during the two unproductive Months, equal to all the preceeding Produce of the Year. A daring Imposition! destitute even of the Degree of Plausibility which is required in Fiction! So gross an Artifice could not deceive for an Instant. But the Presidency proceeded with Caution; and it was not until a direct Confession of the whole Imposture was received from the Chief himself, that the Gentlemen of Ganjam were removed from their Stations (*q*).

This is by no Means the only Instance of Prevarication (*r*), of which the Gentlemen of Ganjam stand convicted. YET, it is ranked among the

---

(*o*) See the Ganjam Cash Accounts on the Company's Records. See also my Minute, App. 2d Rep. No. 60.

(*p*) See my Minutes, App. 2d Rep. No. 60, 61.—Where it is clearly shewn, that the Collections from the Time the Company took Possession of the Ganjam District, to the 30th April, 1779, amounted to one Million, 298,404 : 13 : 27 Pagodas; the Civil and Military Charges during that Period, and Expence of Fortifications, amounted to 976,161 : 10 : 40 Pagodas, exclusive of the Assistance received from the Bengal Troops sent into that District, and also exclusive of the Military Stores sent from the Presidency of Fort St. George. These Calculations are formed from the Company's Records.—From the Amount of the Collections must further be deducted the Sum fallaciously brought to Account by the Gentlemen of Ganjam.

(*q*) See Ganjam Accounts on the Records of the Company for that Period.

(*r*) The Gentlemen of Ganjam declared solemnly, that they did not encourage Ball Kistnah directly or indirectly in his Disobedience, to the Orders of Council, summoning him to Madras; yet in a Letter to Ball Kistnah, in my Possession, in the Hand Writing of one of the Council at Ganjam, he is not only strongly advised to remain in the Country, but the Excuses offered by the Zemindars, for absenting themselves, are suggested to them in the very Words they afterwards adopted. See my App. No. 10.

the foremost of my Offences, That I did not consent to be governed by " the *Representations* of those Gentlemen!"—YET, the Court of Directors have received Mr. Smith and Mr. Johnson into their Favor; for no assigned Reason, but because they were influenced by those Representations (*s*)! YET, the Evidence of those convicted Gentlemen, and of the Gentlemen of the other Subordinates, and of Mr. Smith and Mr. Johnson, who had themselves been Chiefs of Subordinates,—all actuated by the same Passions,—all, though in different Degrees, urged by the same Spirit of Resentment, and biassed by the same Sense of an immediate personal Interest, in fixing a general Odium upon MY Conduct, and in discrediting the greater Part of the Measures of my Administration,—YET, I say, the Evidence, such as I have stated it—The Evidence of Witnesses, who might fairly be challenged on the Trial of a common Issue in Westminster-Hall (*t*)—*This* Evidence is the *sole Foundation* not only of all the Calumny, which has been so busily employed to prejudice my Character in the World, but (what is more serious and affecting) of all the Charges and Imputations which seem to have received the Sanction of the Secret Committee.

Such are the Grounds upon which " it has been thought proper " to advert to my private Transactions (*u*);" to explore, and to publish to the World, the minutest Circumstances of my Affairs; and to call

---

(*s*) This is the *only* Reason assigned by the Court of Directors for their Commendation of Mr. Smith and Mr. Johnson, and for the Lenity of the Sentence passed upon them. See App. 2d Rep. No. 153. Par. 161. It is therefore to be supposed that the same Reason operated to restore them to their Seats in Council.

(*t*) It is by no Means my Intention to impeach generally the Characters of Gentlemen who have served in the Subordinate Councils. I only assert, that interested Parties would not be admitted as Witnesses in a Court of Justice.

(*u*) The Report in enumerating the various Circumstances, which led to this Discussion of my private Transactions, recapitulates several Points, into which I have entered fully in the Course of this Chapter, and, I hope, to the Satisfaction of the Secret Committee, and the Public. It may be necessary, however, to make an additional Remark upon one Subject. " *No Balances* were paid, says the Report, " but *Teeps* (or Draughts) granted for Pagodas " 130,000." The Revenue is never paid, but by Soucars (or Bankers) Bills, called Teeps. I could not alter the established Mode, but I objected to it. See my Minute, App. 2d Rep. No. 49. The Amount of the Balances thus paid at Madras, was a fourth of the Balances due from the Zemindars when they came to the Presidency. As to " the " Terms on which the other Counties were " let," it will be sufficient to observe here, that the Revenue was *raised*, under my Administration, in two of the great Divisions of the Circars; and raised as high as the Zemindars could bear. In the third District, which was absolutely ruined, regardless of a nominal Revenue, I laid the Foundation of a real Production. See my App. No. 11.—After all, Success must depend solely upon the *Fidelity* of the Subordinates.

call upon my confidential Agents and Friends, to reveal the Secrets of their Truſt. Let us ſee whether the Importance of the Diſcoveries, which have reſulted from this Inquiry, will either juſtify the Novelty of the Proceeding, or ſtrengthen the Suſpicion which gave Riſe to it. The Teſtimony of the firſt Witneſs at leaſt, although of conſiderable Length, does not appear to carry with it the Degree of Weight which the Occaſion demanded. I ſhall follow it at large.

The Secret Committee obſerve, " That Captain Foxall informed " them, that he had carried ſome Treaſure to China on Sir Thomas " Rumbold's Account, and that this Treaſure was not entered in the " Book kept by the Officer on Board, called the Boatſwain's Book:" They add further, " That upon examining all the Boatſwain's Books " of the different Ships which had carried Sir Thomas Rumbold's " Treaſure from Madras to China, it appeared, that no Entry or " Delivery of it had been made in any one of them, although the " public Treaſure ſhipped by the Company was entered and delivered " with all neceſſary Particularity (w)."

I ſhall beg Leave to add, that Captain Foxall alſo informed the Committee, " That ſuch Omiſſions are *ſo very frequent*, that he did " not even *enquire why* this Treaſure was not entered in the Book (x)." It is remarkable, that this is the only material Part of the Captain's Evidence, which is not cited in the Report.

The *Company's Treaſure* is always carefully entered in the Ship's Book; becauſe, an Omiſſion there could not eſcape Detection and Cenſure. An equal Attention ought undoubtedly to be paid to the Property of Individuals. Let the Captains excuſe, if they can, their own Neglects. It ſurely does not belong to me, to Account for an Omiſſion, of which I have Reaſon to complain. If the Report means to convey an Idea, that this Omiſſion has an Appearance of Myſtery on my Part; if it is ſuppoſed to be the Effect of any Contrivance of mine, in order to conceal my Property, I ſhall deſire that the Officers belonging to all the Ships in Queſtion, may be examined as to this Point. In the mean Time, I beg Leave to ſubmit myſelf to the common Senſe of the Public. What Sort of Secret is this? which in the

firſt.

(w) See 2d Rep. Page 19.   (x) See App. 2d Rep. No. 63.

first Instance, is intrusted to my own Servants; then to the Captain, from whom I received a Bill of Lading; then to the Purser, who weighed the Money; then to the Mate, who received it into the Ship; then to the Board in China; then to the Consignee; and *lastly*, to *the Court of Justice*, in which I institute a Suit for the Recovery of a Part of the Property which disappeared (*y*).

I return to the Report: " Sir Thomas Rumbold's Solicitor, it ap-
" peared, had demanded Reparation from him (Captain Foxall)
" for his Loss, in April or May 1781. He (Foxall) told your Com-
" mittee, that he had twice called on Sir Thomas Rumbold, since
" his Return from Spain, (1st January 1781) where he (Foxall) had
" been a Prisoner; but had not seen him at either of those Times.
" That Sir Thomas Rumbold had returned his Visit, and saw him;
" but that no Conversation on this Subject then passed."

These Circumstances, however minute, and indeed trivial in Appearance, must doubtless be connected with some Conclusions of grave and important Consequence; otherwise they would hardly have been referred to in a *Part* of the Report, which, aiming without Reserve, a direct Blow against my Honour and Fortune, seemed to promise more than ordinary Weight in the Matter, and more than common Seriousness in the Mode of the Attack. I am therefore infinitely distressed, that my Memory should not serve me to recall either the Ceremonial or the Number of the Visits in Question. It is most certain, that I did not *dun* Captain Foxall. Having once put the Business into the Hands of my Solicitor, I conceive myself as little liable to the Imputation of Guilt, as of Indelicacy, if, in my Interview with that Gentleman, I avoided touching upon the obnoxious Subject.

" Since that Time however," says the Report, " about a Fortnight
" before his (Foxall's) Examination, he had of his own Accord
" waited on Sir Thomas, and represented to him, that he was un-
" able to repay the Loss, having lost 3000l. by his late Capture. To
" which Sir Thomas answered, that he was sorry, but that the
" Money

(*y*) See App. 2d Rep. No. 63.

"Money belonged in Part to Sir Hector Monro, without saying how
"much (z)."

Without being able to recollect precisely every Particular of this Conversation, and without any Knowledge of some of the Facts here alluded to, I at present see no Reason for disputing the Truth of these Assertions.

The Remainder of Captain Foxall's Evidence consists of a Declaration, "That the whole Treasure on Board his Ship, amounted to
"12 or 13,000l. and that the Half had been stolen. That several
"other Ships besides his own, had sailed about the same Time from
"Madras to China. That Captain Prince of the Latham, had told
"him of his having a little Treasure on Board for Sir Thomas
"Rumbold. That he had made a Mistake as to the Number of
"Chests, for that one of them belonged to a Mr. Ferguson. And
"that Mr. Pigou, was Consignee of the Treasure shipped with
"him (a)."

The State of the Consignments made to Mr. Pigou, on my Account, shall be considered presently. With Respect to an Observation cited from this Gentleman, "That above a Million of Money was lying
"in the Hands of Chinese Merchants, belonging to British Sub-
"jects (b)," I shall only say, that a similar Observation might, with equal Truth perhaps, certainly with equal Relation to the Condition of my Fortune, have been extended to the Bank of Venice.

The Report at length proceeds to an Observation of serious Importance. "Your Committee has already stated, that Sir Thomas
"Rumbold, by his third Covenant, had bound himself to deliver
"in to the Board upon Oath, a Particular *of all Loans formerly*
"*made*, and of all Merchandise on Hand, before he should proceed
"to recover the one, or dispose of the other. Upon an accurate
"Examination of the Proceedings of the Board, during the whole
"of Sir Thomas Rumbold's Government, *no Proceeding to that Effect,*
"*was to be found* (c)."

The

(z) See 2d Rep. Page 19.   (b) Ibid. Page 20.
(a) Ibid. Pages 19, 20,   (c) Ibid.

The Reader will remark that the Obligations of the Covenant are here represented by the Secret Committee to be two-fold, and to extend, First, *to all Loans formerly made*; Secondly, to all Merchandise on Hand.—But when he is informed that no such Article, as the *First*, does in Reality exist in the Covenant; and that no such Merchandise as is referred to in the *Second*, remained to be disposed of;—he will, I hope, cease to be surprised that " no Proceedings to " the Effect," expected by the Secret Committee, " should appear " on the Records of the Presidency."

In the Covenant in Question, there are two Accounts required to be delivered in by me, as President of Fort St. George, within thirty Days after my Arrival at Madras. First, a List of Debts then owing to me, in the Course of Trade and Commerce, and of the Goods, Wares, Merchandise and Stock in Trade then remaining to me.—— *Secondly*—An Account of all *such* Loan or Loans (if any) as I *stood concerned* in, *with any of the Country Powers in India, or with any Persons holding Commissions under them* (*d*).

It is needless to point out the Difference between *this* State of the Obligations in the Covenant, and *that* which the Report has held out to the Public, in the last cited Passage;—in which, the Limitation of my Engagements, the Description of the particular Kind of Loans for which alone I was bound to account, is totally and inexplicably *omitted*.

It is of more Consequence to assure the Public, upon the Evidence of my *Books* (*e*), *delivered in to the Secret Committee*, that as long ago as the Year 1772, my Accounts in Trade were finally closed, except some Trifling Articles, which were adjusted in the subsequent Years.—That my whole Property in India, at the Date of the Covenant in Question, consisted in Bonds and Notes due to me from the Company, and from European Individuals settled at *Bengal*. And that I had no Concern with the Country Powers, or their Agents.

(*d*) See the Covenant. App. 2d Rep. No. 2.   (*e*) See App. 2d Rep. No. 56.

The Report proceeds, " Your Committee has alſo ſtated, That in the ſame Covenant, he had bound himſelf to receive no Emolument whatever, except the Salary and Perquiſites ſpecified therein, which have been ſtated to amount to 18 or perhaps £.20,000 per Annum: YET the Committee find, that between the 8th February (the Day of his Arrival) *and the Beginning of Auguſt,* Sir Thomas Rumbold had ſhipped the following Sums from Madras to China.

	Pagodas	£.
" By the Latham	50,000	20,000
" By the Hillſborough	50,000	20,000
" By the Royal George (Part of Sir H. Munro's)	39,000	13,000
	Dollars	
" By the Seahorſe	20,000	5,000
	(*f*)	£. 58,000

In ſpeaking to this Account, I muſt begin with ſtriking out the laſt Article; in doing which, I ſhall be ſupported by an Authority, that will hardly be conteſted by the Secret Committee. In the *very ſame Page,* of the Second Report, in which is exhibited the above recited Statement of my Remittances to China, *in the Year one Thouſand Seven Hundred and Seventy* EIGHT, we read the following Words. " Mr. Pigou being examined as to the Conſignments from " Madras in *One Thouſand Seven Hundred and Seventy* NINE, ſaid, " that by the Seahorſe, 20,000 Dollars were remitted for Sir Thomas " Rumbold (*g*)!"

By this Article, the Committee have relieved me from the Neceſſity of proving that in the Year Seventeen Hundred and Seventy EIGHT, the Seahorſe was employed under Sir Edward Vernon at the Siege of Pondicherry, and did not go to China, until *September* Seventeen Hundred and Seventy NINE.

Thus my Remittances to China, between the Months of February and Auguſt in the Year Seventeen Hundred and Seventy EIGHT, are reduced to 53,000 l. From this Sum again, 12,000 l. muſt be deducted

(*f*) See 2d Rep. Page 20. (*g*) Ibid.

ducted on account of Sir Hector Munro, who was interested to that Amount in the Remittance.

Now to account for my having been able, in the short Space of Six Months, to make a Remittance to the Amount of this reduced Sum of 41,000l, without having Recourse to the *Supposition* of illicit Practices, and Breach of Covenant, I must beg Leave to state (and for the Truth of this I refer to the Company's Records) that at the Time of making these Remittances, there had accrued on account of the Commission on Coral, and on account of my Salary, (which took Place from the Day of my leaving England) a Sum amounting nearly to nineteen thousand Pounds.

Thus the Part of the Remittances remaining to be accounted for, is reduced to a Sum, which is more than *balanced* (as appears in a Statement in the Appendix to the second Report No. 66) by the Sums of 14,000 Pagodas, which I borrowed of Mrs. Casamajor, and of 30,000 Pagodas borrowed from Chickapoore Chitty, and other black Merchants; by other Articles of inferior Moment, stated in the same Number of the Appendix: and by Bills drawn by me upon Bengal, and Remittances received from thence, to the Amount of upwards of 14,000l. Sterling.

I voluntarily submitted to the Inspection of the Secret Committee, all the Accounts that were saved from the General Barker, and consented to their Publication. These Accounts, which serve as Explanations of my Remittances, exhibit the State of my Fortune in Bengal, in the Year 1772. The Remittances however, it should be remarked, are brought forward to the public Eye, in the Body of the Report; while the Pieces which account for, and justify their Amount, are to be sought in the Appendix. It appears that my Estate in India at the Period referred to (1772) amounted to near ten Lacks of Rupees; *exclusive of Interest on many Accounts not adjusted,*—which last Circumstance is omitted in the Report.—I am therefore at a Loss to discover upon what Ground either of Reason or Candour, it can be held out as a Subject of public Admiration or Concern, that in the Years 1778 and 1779, my Remittances *on my own Account*, should amount to about 130,000l. (*h*) Sterling; since it

(*h*) The whole of my Remittances amounted to £. 167,019 19 4.—But of this Sum £. 38,091 13 was remitted on Account of other People.

it is apparent that my Means of making thofe Remittances, arifing from a Fortune acquired long before, were more than proportioned to the Sum remitted; and fince it is well known, that one of my principal Objects in foliciting the Appointment to the Government of Fort St. George, was the being placed in a Situation which might afford me Opportunities of remitting my Property to my native Country.

But the Court of Directors, it feems, are of a different Opinion. A Fortune of One hundred thoufand Pounds, vefted at -Intereft for feveral Years, in their own Securities, and thofe of their European Servants in Bengal, hardly attracts their Attention. Their Logic is of a Piece with their Equity; and it was worthy of both, to turn their Eyes from the fubftantial Funds, of which I was avowedly pof- feffed, in order to trace fome By-Channel of Refource, in a Scrap of the Will of a difcarded Secretary, or in a Warrant of Arreft iffuing from their Mayor's Court at Madras.

" Another Circumftance of a *fingular* Nature," fays the Report,
" was found on the Proceedings of the Mayor's Court at Madras.
" The late Mr. Redhead had been Secretary to Sir Thomas Rumbold,
" and died at Madras. His Executors after his Death, obtained a
" Warrant of Arreft againft Setteram Rauze, for the Balance of
" 70,000 Rupees, promifed to Mr. Redhead; but no Step appears
" to have been taken by the Members of Government to prevent
" this, nor are the Directors made acquainted with it by them (*i*).

The fecret Committee, I am perfuaded, are by this Time better informed of the State of Abufes in India: Nor, can I conceive that if the fecond Report were now to be compiled, they would confider the Tranfaction, the Exiftence of which is inferred from the Cir- cumftance here ftated, as being *fingular* in its Nature. In one great Inftance, I ftruck at the Root of thofe Abufes. The Return I have met with, at the Hands of the Court of Directors, will hardly en- courage others to adventure in the fame Line. To fay the Truth, a thorough Reform in this Branch, how effential foever to the Welfare of India, to the Profperity of the Company, to the Dignity and Refources

(*i*) See 2d Rep. Page 20.

sources of the Nation, is not likely to be seriously attempted, as long as the Direction at Home shall remain in its present State. Such a Reform, by reducing the Value of Patronage, would too sensibly affect the Importance and the Interests of the Patrons.

With respect to Mr. Redhead, I shall touch with Delicacy upon the Memory of a Person, who cannot now be heard in his Defence. He was not in the Service of the Company. He was my private Secretary; but he had ceased to be in my Confidence, for some Time before the Arrival of the Zemindars, and was finally dismissed from his Employment, long before the Conclusion of the Agreement with them. The Letter of Dismission was dated the 11th of August 1778, and can be produced by his Executors. He died in September or October following.

With respect to the Warrant of Arrest, issued by the Mayor's Court, against Setteram Rauze, at the Suit of Mr. Redhead's Executors; what Steps would the Secret Committee have recommended to the Presidency, in order to prevent it? They cannot be ignorant of the general Censure which the Bengal Government incurred long ago, by the Suspicion of such an Interference with the regular Course of Justice; nor can they be uninformed of the Measures pursued by the Legislature upon that Subject. A Transaction of the Mayor's Court, could not come legally before the Presidency. The Truth is, the Transaction in Question was lost amidst the Multiplicity of Affairs continually agitating in that Court, and did not come under the View of the Presidency in any Sense, until an Appeal was preferred before them, from one of the Decisions of the Mayor's Court in this Business, when the Decision was reversed. The Proceedings of the Court of Appeals are regularly transmitted to the Court of Directors.

OBSERVATIONS

ON THE

SUPPLEMENT

TO THE

SECOND REPORT

OF THE

SECRET COMMITTEE.

THE Supplement to the Second Report opens with a Correspondence, and with the Opinions of Mr. Sadlier, when Chief of Mazulipatam, on the Measure of Calling up the Zemindars to the Presidency. It is of Importance to remark, that when Mr. Sadlier offered his Opinions upon that Subject, he was too young in his Office to have formed them on the Basis of Experience and Observation. Neither should it be overlooked, that the Tendency of

Mr.

Mr. Sadlier's Advice seems to have been rather prudential than political. Aware of the desperate Condition of the Finances, and foreseeing that Mischiefs, long before accomplished, would be imputed to the Change of System I was introducing, he expresses much Apprehension for the *Credit* of *my* Government. " May not " the Effects of former improper Management," says he, " be ascribed " to the present Plan? If the Settlement is on the Decline, would it " not be *prudent* to leave the Government *hitherto* charged with Re-" sponsibility, *to justify* its Measures,—and bear the *Censure it* " *deserves* (a)?"

In yielding to these Suggestions, I should, doubtless, have consulted my personal Ease, and have escaped the Persecutions to which I have since been exposed. But I should have betrayed my Trust,—and *justly* have incurred the Censure of having paid no Attention to a Communication of a *most confidential Nature*, contained in a *private* Letter from Mr. Sadlier of the same Date. This Letter professedly written, " *in Proof of Confidence*," I have never thought myself at Liberty to divulge. I much doubt whether Mr. Sadlier will stand justified in the Opinions of Men of Feeling, for having published (*b*) so *confidential* a Letter, although written by himself; especially as he has not thought proper to give it entire and unmutilated. The Letter, and the Papers it enclosed, are still in my Possession; and as Mr. Sadlier has now released me from every Obligation to Secrecy, I shall here submit the suppressed Passage to the Secret Committee, and to the Public. The Contents of this Passage will not, I believe, be

thought

(*a*) See Supplement to 2d Rep. Page 11.

(*b*) The *Grounds* on which Mr. Sadlier's public Virtue is founded, will appear in an extraordinary Point of View, when the Intelligence contained in the following Extract of a Letter, addressed to me by a Member of the Council of Madras, shall have been properly weighed.

Extract of a Letter from Madras, dated 15th January, 1781.

" Mr. Smith (the Governor) asked Mr. " William Rofs, in consequence of what he " said, viz. *That Mr. Sadlier would suppress* " *the Information, if he were reinstated with* " *the Participation of General Coote*, whether " such Message were delivered by Mr. Sad-" lier's Authority? Mr. Rofs said, No: But " he knew it to be Mr. Sadlier's Intention. " Mr. Smith desired Mr. Rofs to go back to " Mr. Sadlier, to know from him his Inten-" tion. Mr. Rofs returned, (this was the " 11th Instant) and told Mr. Smith, Mr. Sad-" lier said, *That if he were reinstated, he gave* " *his Word of Honour, the Informations should* " *be suppressed, and never appear at any future* " *Period*."

thought to come under the Description of "*Official Intelligence* (c)."
—The Passage is as follows. " It was usual before Whitchill's Time
" for the Governor to share †. Whitchill succeeding after Wynch,
" whose Actions had left no Tye but Honour, which with some has
" no Force, for Compliance with Custom,—Whitchill saved such Tax
" —Craufurd, I believe, enjoyed all.—Floyer Chief, Mr. Stratton
" Governor, Brothers in Iniquity, fit to deal with each other, induced
" Floyer to keep all.—This Conduct in Chiefs brought on Opposition
" to their Measures in Council at Madras, which in Effect weakened
" Government here by reversing it's Acts, *and has introduced Distrust in*
" *the Zemindars.*" The Reader will hardly be surprised at the Effect,
said to have been produced upon the Minds of the Zemindars by such
Proceedings. Nor can I think it necessary to add another Word in
Defence of the new System I introduced, as far as it's Operations extended to the Abridgment of the Powers of the Subordinate Councils.

But the Report proceeds, " Your Committee do not find, that the
" *official Intelligence*, communicated by Mr. Sadlier, was made the
" Ground of any *Inquiry* or *Reformation* during the Government of
" Sir Thomas Rumbold (*d*)."

It will no longer, I presume, be urged that the *Intelligence* I received
on this Occasion, was *official.* It was not however neglected. Supported by such Authority, I ventured, with greater Determination,
upon the hazardous Task of *reforming* Abuses ; without thinking myself either authorized in Honour, or justified in Prudence to direct
my Attack to Persons (*e*). I did not even acknowledge the Receipt of

Q Mr.

(*c*) Ibid. Page 17.
(*d*) Ibid. Page 17.
(*e*) It is not pretended that any of the Circumstances referred to, in this *private*, *not* " official, Intelligence," happened during my Government. Mr. Whitchill, after having been Chief of Mazulipatam, had returned to Europe ; and was sent back to India, with extraordinary Marks of the Approbation of the Court of Directors. Mr. Floyer had left Madras, before the Receipt of Mr. Sadlier's Intelligence. Mr. Craufurd had been only temporary Chief. The honourable Court will permit me to observe, that, the two Gentlemen last mentioned, had been leading Members of their FA-
VORITE

Mr. Sadlier's private Letter, as is alledged, by Miftake in the Report (*f*). But I ftated the Nature and Confequences of the Abufes fairly and diftinctly to the Court of Directors, whofe immediate Duty it was to inftitute an Inquiry (*g*). The honourable Court, however, have never expreffed the flighteft Curiofity with refpect to the *Perfons* by whom the Abufes were committed.

I have no where reprefented the Meafure of calling the Zemindars to the Prefidency, as being free from Objection, or unattended with Difficulties. But amidft a Choice of Difficulties, I thought it the leaft liable to Exception. It has certainly not been productive of the Mifchiefs that are afcribed to it:—For, long before any Steps had been taken in this Bufinefs, all Payment either of Tribute or Balances appeared to be hopelefs. And, *if* the Zemindars had the Means of fulfilling their Engagements with the *Company*, the Subordinates muft have wanted the *Will*, for they had the *Power*, to enforce the Performance.

But the Secret Committee give the Preference " to the Mea-
" fure which was ordered by the Court of Directors; namely,
" that a Committee from the Prefidency fhould enquire upon the
" Spot, into every Circumftance which affected the refpective Interefts
" of the Peafants, the Zemindars, and the Company (*h*)"

I fhall not here repeat what I have already urged on this Subject. But I beg Leave to obferve, that, *the Proceedings* of the Committee of Circuit inftituted in BENGAL in 1773, which have probably been concealed from the Secret Committee, ought not to have impreffed the Court of Directors with fo favorable an Opinion, as they feem now to entertain of fuch Inftitutions. The Committee of Circuit in Bengal put up the Dewanny Lands to Auction, and let them, as they faid, to the beft Bidders, for five Years, at a Rent, which was to increafe

VORITE COMMITTEE OF CIRCUIT, inftituted exprefsly, to *controul* the *Subordinates*, and adminifter *Relief to the Natives*.

(*f*) See Supp. Page 16. Mr. Sadlier has declared on Oath, that he received no Anfwer to that Letter. See his Depofition, Supplimental App. No. 3.

(*g*) See my App. No. 1.

(*h*) See Supp. Page 10.

crease annually. At the End of the five Years, however, it appeared that the Remiſſions and Balances on their Settlement amounted to the enormous Sum of two Millions and a Half Sterling.

I beg Leave here to introduce two Paragraphs from different Letters of the Court of Directors to the Governor General and Council, which ſhew plainly what Sort of Facts muſt have come before them, reſpecting the Conduct of the Committee of Circuit, in that Part of India; and what Concluſion they ought to have drawn from thoſe Facts, reſpecting the real Principles and probable Effects of ſuch Appointments.

Extract of the General Letter to the Governor General and Council at Fort William in Bengal, dated 28*th November,* 1777.

Paragraph 30. " We find that the Farm of Sylhet was granted by
" the Committee of Circuit; that the Company's *Advance* to the
" Farmers of Sylhet of 33,000 Rupees for Elephants, was received
" *by one of the Members of that Committee.* It has however ſince ap-
" peared, that the oſtenſible Farmers, or Perſons named in the Com-
" mittee's Settlement, *never exiſted,* and that the Company's Reſident
" at Sylhet, was *the real* Farmer, under fictitious Names."

Extract of the General Letter to the Governor General and Council, at Fort William in Bengal, dated 4*th March,* 1778.

Paragraph 77. " In our Letter of the 5th of February, 1777, you
" were informed, that although it was rather our Wiſh to prevent
" future Evils, than to enter into a ſevere Retroſpection of paſt
" Abuſes, yet as in ſome of the Caſes then before us, *we conceived*
" *there had been flagrant Corruption, and in others great Oppreſſions*
" *committed on the Native Inhabitants,* we thought it unjuſt to ſuffer
" the Delinquents to paſs wholly unpuniſhed, and therefore autho-
" rized you to take ſuch Steps as you might think proper to be pur-
" ſued on the Occaſion, acquainting you, at the ſame time, that we
" ſhould, if neceſſary, return you the original Covenants of thoſe of
" our

"our Servants, who had been concerned in the undue Receipt of
"Money, in order to enable you to recover the same for the Use of
"the Company, and having reconsidered the Subject, *we hereby direct,*
"*that you forthwith commence a Prosecution in the Supreme Court of*
"*Judicature, against the Persons who composed the Committee of*
"*Circuit.*"

But to return to Mr. Sadlier. Another of his Letters is cited in the Report, giving an Account of a Conference that took place between that Gentleman, and Sir Hector Munro, Mr. Whitehill, and myself, on the Eve of my Departure from Madras. I cannot discover any Inference to my Disadvantage that can be drawn from what passed at this Conference, even as stated by Mr. Sadlier himself. Ungentleman-like Language will not, I am sure, be received as Argument by the Secret Committee. Mr. Sadlier is subject to Extremes. At one Moment his Gratitude towards me, the next, his Anger, are alike excessive. It was a principal Object of my Instructions, to restore Harmony in the Settlement, which had been divided into Factions by the unfortunate Revolution of 1776. It was partly with a View to this Object, that I had recommended Mr. Sadlier, in Contradiction to the Sentiments of some Members of the Council, to succeed to the Chiefship of Masulipatam (*i*). I had the good Fortune to establish Peace and Regularity in the Settlement, and to preserve it during the Whole of my Residence at Madras. But there were not wanting the Seeds of future Animosities. And I was so convinced that the Harmony I had with much Difficulty restored, would be interrupted soon after my Departure, that nothing but the positive Declaration of my Physician, who pronounced it to be impossible for me to outlive the Month of May in India, should have induced me to abandon my Government,

---

(*i*) Mr. Sadler had been suspended the Service. His Conduct was submitted to the Court of Directors; but before their Opinion could be received, he was restored by the Interest of the Governor, Mr. Stratton. Although restored, however, he was not permitted to hold the Offices which his Station in the Service entitled him to. I thought it more adviseable to employ him, and accordingly proposed, that he should be appointed to the Chiefship of Mazulipatam. The Grounds of his Suspension are explained, in the Company's Records, in the following Terms.

"Mr. Sadlier, in the Management of the Company's Affairs at Ingeram, has acted prejudicially to the Company, cruelly and oppressively to the Natives, and injuriously to the French and Dutch, who claim the same Privilege with ourselves to make Investments."

vernment, and my Measures, at that important Juncture. Rumours of projected Factions had reached me from various Quarters. A Remonstrance, formally delivered to me by the Gentleman who was to succeed me in the Government, commanded my Attention (*k*). I did not however depart from the usual Mildness of my Administration. I opened my Sentiments to Mr. Sadlier, with Temper and Civility; but I declared to him, without Disguise, that, if I could conceive it to be the View of any Man, to avail himself of a Seat at the Board, to introduce *Factions* and *Disturbances* into the Settlement, I would not hesitate to exert the Powers with which the Company had armed me (*l*), and that I would refuse to call such a Man to his Seat in Council.—Things however were suffered to take their Course, and the Conference broke up, upon the positive Assurance of Mr. Sadlier, that whatever Difference of Opinion might arise, he would in all Occurrences conduct himself with Moderation and Candour.—I shall now take Leave of Mr. Sadlier without Anger, and without Apprehension.

In the 11th and 12th Pages of the Supplement to the 2d Report, the Secret Committee state the Opinions of Mr. Petrie respecting the Abolition of the Committee of Circuit, and calling the Zemindars to the Presidency. But, on these Points, the Opinions of that Gentleman, however respectable in himself, will not be suffered to operate to my Disadvantage, when it is considered that they can only be founded on Hearsay, and probably on the Prejudices of People, whose own Views had been disappointed by the Measures in Question. Mr. Petrie has had no Means of acquiring any Knowledge of the Circars, having always been employed on a different Service.

The Evidence of Mr. Cotsford, which is next stated, has a Claim to greater Attention, as that Gentleman has been much employed to the Northward. It is observable that his Opinion does *not* coincide with that of the Court of Directors, on the Subject of a Committee of Circuit. If, in another Instance, he differs as much from me, it should be considered that he has been *Chief of a Subordinate*, and cannot be supposed to be entirely uninfluenced by the Prejudices of Situ-
R   ation.

(*k*) See my App. No. 12.
(*l*) See Company's Dispatches to Fort St. George, dated 10th April 1773.

ation. It is not to be expected that the Measure of calling the Zemindars to the Presidency, should meet with the Approbation of a subordinate Council.

After what I have said in the preceding Defence on the Subject of Remittances, I do not apprehend that it will be necessary to enter here into an Examination of the additional Evidence on that Subject, produced in the Supplement to the second Report. I shall only offer a Remark on one Passage, which seems to convey an Idea that I had deceived the Committee with respect to Sir Hector Munro's Share of those Remittances.

The Committee say, that " Matthew Raper, Esq; another Super-
" cargo, confirmed Captain Foxall and Mr. Pigou's Account respect-
" ing the Sum stated in the 2d Report (Page 20) to have been paid
" in to him and his Partner, on *Sir Thomas Rumbold's Account*—and
" *proved*, that the Portion belonging to Sir Hector Munro, was of
" the Value of £466 : 10 : 3 (*m*)." There needs only a Reference to the supplemental Appendix to the 2d Report, No. 2, to clear up this Mistake of the Committee.

Mr. Raper's Evidence is as follows:—" The only Transaction for
" Sir Thomas Rumbold was relating to 25,000 Pagodas—the Produce
" of which I remitted myself: it was ordered to be paid to me
" and Mr. Cromlin by Bradshaw and Pigou, on Sir Thomas's Ac-
" count; this was the latter End of 1778. Mr. Cromlin being ab-
" sent at the Time the Money was remitted, I sent it in my own
" Name by a Bill on the Company in January 1779, payable to
" Robert Mackrith, John Stables, and Thomas Raikes, Esquires,
" amounting to £10,769 : 12 : 11 (*n*)." I must observe that the half of this Sum was on Account of Sir Hector Munro (*o*), and has been regularly paid to his Attornies in England, Mr. Duncan Davidson and others; as well as a further Sum of the China Remittance, the Receipts for which Sum on his Account are in my Possession. The other Part of Mr. Raper's Evidence, is as follows:

" I had

(*m*) See Supp. Page 13. (*o*) See my App. No. 13.
(*n*) Ibid. Page 2.

" I had a Consignment from Madras to China, belonging to
" Sir Hector Munro, of Dollars amounting to £466 : 10 : 3 (*p*),"
This is a separate Sum of which I have not the least Knowledge,
and yet it is said by the Committee of Secrecy, to be proved to be
the Portion belonging to Sir Hector Munro, of the Sum, stated *in
Mr. Pigou's Evidence*, to have been paid to Mr. Matthew Raper,
and his Partner Mr. Cromlin.

With respect to " the further Light afforded to the Committee,
" by the Testimony of Mr. Petrie, respecting the Present of a Lack
" of Rupees, stated in the 2d Report (page 20) to have been se-
" cured to Mr. Redhead, by Setteram Rauze (*q*) ;" I can add nothing
to what I have already offered on that Subject. It may not, however, be improper to remark that whatever Agreement Mr. Redhead
might presume to enter into with Setteram Rauze, it does not appear that he is even *supposed* to have fulfilled in any Degree *his*
Part of the Agreement, since the latter contests the Payment of
the Money.

(*p*) See Supp. No. 2.   (*q*) Ibid. Page 13.

OBSERVATIONS

ON THE

FOURTH REPORT.

I Procede to the FOURTH REPORT, which contains some Particulars respecting the Revenues of the Company on the Coast, that are connected with my Administration.

The Committee in the 5th Page of the 4th Report, state " The
" Balances of the Madras Treasury at different Periods, for the four
" last Years, ending the 25th March 1780.——

" 30th June 1777,   Pagodas 429,552,   £ 171,820
" 31st January 1778,   557,794,   143,117
" 28th January 1779,   236,916,   94,766
" 25th March 1780,   288,238,   115,295"

The Committee then observe, " That from the Difference in the
" Periods, no very great Comparison can be made of the State of the
" Treasury, in these respective Years, but so far your Committee
" think themselves warranted to observe, from this Account, that,
" on the 25th March 1780, the State of the Treasury was not such
" as upon Comparison with its Situation at other Periods, implied
" any particular Attention to that Object." Let the Correspondence between the Presidency of Fort St. George, and the Court of Directors,

as well as that between the same Presidency and the Governor-General and Council be brought forward, and they will prove that continual Representations have been made at all Periods, respecting the Lowness of the Madras Treasury, and the Impossibility of replenishing it from the Resources on the Coast, which could barely support a Peace Establishment. They will prove also, that notwithstanding the heavy Expences incurred by the Siege and Reduction of Pondicherry, by the Reduction of Mahé, by the Maintenance of French Prisoners, by the transporting them from the Coast, by compleating the Fortifications of Fort St. George (*a*), by the Expedition, sent *reluctantly* from Madras, in Support of the fatal Maratta War (an Accumulation of Difficulties, which no other Governor has had to contend with) only twenty Lacks of Rupees were received from Bengal during my Administration, to relieve our Necessities; and *that*, in Consequence of frequent Applications and Remonstrances. These Remittances were sent in Gold to be coined in the Madras Mint; which occasioned a considerable Loss upon the Remittance. Let it be observed further, that, during the Course of these Difficulties, the Investments of the Company suffered no Interruption (*b*). When the Court of Directors shall be compelled to produce the Records of the India House, fully and fairly, the Praise of Activity, Zeal, and Integrity, will no longer be refused to my Administration.

At no Period during the Course of eight Years, was the Nabob's Debt to the Company so much reduced, as at the Close of my Government. The Nabob's Debt the 15th March, 1780, is stated to be   Pagodas (*c*)   5,92,447 34 21
From which must be deducted, received 31st March,
                                Pagodas 85,800
Received 2d April   -   -   3,200   89,000
I quitted the Government the 6th April 1780, when
the Nabob's Debt was reduced to (*d*)   5,03,447 34 21

His

(*a*) See Letter from the chief Engineer, in my App. No. 14.
(*b*) The most considerable and valuable Part of the Company's Investment, is provided from the Districts, under the Factory of Vizagapatam. The Investment from the Mazulipatam District, is but trifling in Comparison. For Proof that the Investment under Vizagapatam, was amply supplied, see Letter from the Chief and Council, App. 2d Rep. No. 54.
(*c*) See 4th Rep. Page 73.
(*d*) See the Company's Treasury Accounts to the 6th of April 1780, the Date of my Resignation.

His Debt for the seven preceding Years, amounted, one Year with another, to Pagodas 700,000 (*e*). The Nabob, *at the Time I quitted the Government*, was not at all, or but little indebted to the Company for " any Lands leased to Him (*f*)."

The Rajah of Tanjour had nearly paid up the Arrears of his Subsidy (*g*). I beg Leave here to offer an Observation relative to the Rajah of Tanjour. The Committee of Secrecy observe " That Governor Rumbold, in a Letter to the Rajah, dated August 6th 1779, " charges him with being very backward in his Payments, and writes, " that one Lack of Pagodas was due for the June preceding. The " Rajah in his Answer, dated 3d September, 1779, vindicates " himself from the Charge, and by a Statement of Accounts shews, " that he had paid in full for the three Years for which his Agree-" ment with the Company had subsisted, and, that he was 56,000 " Pagodas in Advance (*h*)."

I am concerned, that Copies of my Letter to the Rajah and his Answer, have not been given in the Appendix to the Report. The Committee of Secrecy have not taken Notice, in any Part of their Reports, that, independent of his Subsidy, the Rajah had agreed, before my Government, to deposit four Lacks of Pagodas in the Company's Treasury, to remain there until certain Claims of the Nabob, and all Disputes between them, should be settled. Of this Deposit, he only paid one Lack of Pagodas; and never could be prevailed on to pay any more. He afterwards was desirous, that this one Lack of Pagodas should be carried to the Credit of his Subsidy; which I did not think myself authorised to allow. Here then will be found the Explanation of the Difference between the Rajah's Account and mine.

It

(*e*) See 4th Rep. Page 73.
(*f*) It will be proved fully, when we come to consider the Business of the Jagheer, not only that the Nabob incurred no new Debt during my Government, for " any Lands " leased to him;" but that he even acquitted Arrears which were due when I arrived at the Presidency.—In the mean Time, see my App. No. 15.
(*g*) See the Company's Treasury Accounts to the 5th of April 1780—And my App. No. 15.
(*h*) See 4th Rep. Page 74.

[68]

It will be neceffary for me to enter a little more minutely into the Account of the Progrefs of encreafing Balances from the Northern Circars (as ftated in Page 44, of the 4th Report)—The Committee of Secrecy fay, " Your Committee, in the Courfe of their Enquires into
" the Receipt of the Revenues under the Prefidency of Madras, could
" not but obferve the very large Arrears due by the Renters, and
" other Pofleffors of Lands, and which appear to have rapidly increafed
" of late, particularly in the Northern Circars: and your Committee,
" being defirous of afcertaining the Progrefs of thefe Balances, called
" for a particular State of them, *as they flood at the refpective Termi-*
" *nations* of the Governments of Lord Pigot, Mr. Stratton, Mr.
" Whitehill, and Sir Thomas Rumbold, *and at the Date of the laft*
" *Advices*; in Obedience to which, the following Account was pro-
" duced."

" At the End of Lord Pigot's Government, 24th Auguft, 1776.

			Pagodas.
" Mafulipatam	- Northern Circars	- -	2,79,604
" Vizagapatam	- Northern Circars	- -	72,203
" Ganjam	- Northern Circars	- -	2,71,672

6,23,79

" At the End of Mr. Stratton's Goverment, 31ft Auguft, 1777.

" Mafulipatam	- Northern Circars	- -	2,50,942
" Vizagapatam	- Northern Circars	- -	2,52,858
" Ganjam	- Northern Circars	- -	3,21,909

8,25,709

" At the End of Mr. Whitehill's Government, 7th February, 1778.

" Mafulipatam	- Northern Circars	- -	3,84,283
" Vizagapatam	- Northern Circars	- -	1,93,891
" Ganjam	- Northern Circars .	- -	3,77,021

9,55,195

" Sir Thomas Rumbold refigned the Government of Madras the 4th
" of April, 1780, the laſt Accounts received of the Balances due
" from the Circars, are dated the 29th of February, 1780; at
" which Time they ſtood as follows :

" Maſulipatam   - Northern Circars   -   -   9,92,926
" Vizagapatam   - Northern Circars   -   -   3,24,156
" Ganjam   - Northern Circars   -   -   4,02,482
                                                 ─────────
                                                 17,19,600"

No juſt Idea can be formed of the Progreſs of the Balances, without clearly underſtanding the Principle on which the Accounts ought to be made out. It is a Rule at the Preſidency of Madras to Debit the Subordinates for the Amount Revenue as it *appears* to become due by the *Agreements* with the Zemindars ; and Credit is not given to the Subordinates, until the *Accounts* of the Collections, and Diſburſements, *have been received*. Theſe *Accounts* are ſometimes not tranſmitted to the Preſidency for one, two, or three Months ; conſequently the Zemindars or Subordinates, ſtand *Debited*, in the Statements ſent to Europe, and Balances appear againſt them, which do not exiſt. For the Statement of Balances can only be adjuſted with *accuracy* in the General Books, cloſed always the 30th April, in each Year. I ſhall therefore take the Liberty to bring the ſeveral Accounts to their *proper Periods*, ſtill adopting the Statement of Payments, given by the Secret Committee, in Pages 18 and 19 of the fourth Report.

1ſt. From the 30th April 1776 to the 30th April 1777, the Balance due at the latter Period.

Northern Circars, Land Revenues   Pagodas 575,053.

2d. From the 30th April 1777 to the 30th April 1778, the Balance due at the latter Period.

Northern Circars, Land Revenues   Pagodas 1,190,213.

[70]

It was this laft alarming State of Balances, added to a Sufpenfion of all Payment, and the Critical Situation of Affairs, that induced me to propofe the Meafure of calling the Zemindars to the Prefidency. But it muft be obferved, that the Orders for the Zemindars coming to Madras, were not iffued *until the 15th* April 1778; that none of them left their Diftricts *until the latter end of May*: that their Accounts ought to have been fettled; and the Books clofed the 30th April: and confequently that the Meafure in queftion could not *be the Caufe* of this laft cited ftate of *Arrears* which had accrued before I interfered in the Adminiftration of the Circars.

3d. From the 30th April 1778, to the 30th April 1779, the Balance due at the latter Period (*i*),

NORTHERN CIRCAR, Land Revenues   -   Pagodas 1,350,996.

No Books are yet received ftating the Revenue from the 30th April 1779, to the 30th April 1780, the greater Part of which Period was in my Government. The Committee indeed ftate the Balances on the 29th February 1780 (Page 41 of 4th Report) to amount to Pagodas 17,17,600, this muft be taken from the laft *Accounts received at the Prefidency from the Subordinates*. The Amount collected from the Date of that Account to the 30th April, remains to be deducted; which will make a confiderable Change in the State of Balances, as the Collection in the Mafulipatam Diftrict (very different from that of Ganjam) is chiefly made in the Months of March and April. The Amount of Teeps muft alfo be deducted, as being no longer a Balance on the Country. It muft be obferved alfo, that the Zemindars of Mafulipatam had been allowed *four Years* to liquidate their Balances, at the Recommendation of the Chief and Council of that Factory. And it muft be further obferved that there was an Increafe on the Tribute from September 1778. viz.

MASULIPATAM, Lands and Farms, about   Pagodas 40,000.

VIZAGAPATAM, Lands 131,000 Rupees, or   37,400

Annual Increafe,   - - -   Pagodas 77,400

This

(*i*) Lord Pigot took Charge of the Government, the 9th December 1775; was removed from it the 24th Auguft 1776, when Mr. Stratton fucceeded. Mr.

This Increase of the stipulated Tribute, from the Neglects of the Subordinates, or the real Distresses of the Country, instead of adding to the Revenue, has only served to swell the Balances in an increased Proportion. Had the Tribute remained at the Rate of former Assessments, the Balances would have been proportionably less. Mr. Cotsford, in his Evidence before the Committee, treats this Increase of the Tribute in the Masulipatam District, as " an injudicious " Measure." But I have been censured by the Court of Directors, and have been very severely dealt with, on a Supposition that I had suffered the Tribute to be under-rated. What would they have said or done, if I had *reduced* the Tribute, which perhaps would have been the most advisable Step? I shall not enter into an Enquiry, why a larger Amount has not been collected, since the Settlement made under my Government. It is certain that the Chief and Council of Masulipatam in their Letter to the Presidency in March 1780, speak with Confidence of their Prospect of receiving the whole Amount due from all the Tributaries (*k*): And the President and Council in their Letters, from the Civil and Revenue Department to the Court of Directors, of the 9th January 1780, condemn the Chief and Council of Mazulipatam, for not having exerted themselves, as much as they might and ought to have done (*l*). The Committee of Secrecy observe, (Page 45, fourth Report) That the Balances due from the Zemindars and Renters, under Masulipatam alone, are said to amount, *including Teeps due*, to no less than Madras Pagodas 1,528,597,17. The *amount Teeps* must however be deducted. The Remainder only can be considered as a Balance on the Country.

With Respect to the Chicacole Circar, the Letter from the Presidency of Madras, of the 7th of January, 1781 (*m*), and a Letter received by me from Mr. Casamajor, the Chief of Vizagapatam (*n*), shew, that the Whole of the Balances from that District, which is stated (Page 44, fourth Report) to amount to Pagodas 324,156, would *soon* be collected (*o*). In all the Districts every Thing depends

on

Mr. Stratton held the Government till September 1777; Mr. Whitehill, from that Period, to the 8th February 1778, when I succeeded, and left it in April 1780.

(*k*) See my App. No. 8.

(*l*) See Supp. App. to 2d Rep. No. 7, 8.
(*m*) Ibid. No. 8.
(*n*) See my App. No. 6.
(*o*) Briefly thus. When I entered upon my Government, (1778) the Balances amounted
to

on the Conduct of the Subordinates. I never supposed the Balances could be collected in the Mazulipatam District, but by allowing Time, and affording the Zemindars every proper Indulgence; for they certainly are distressed in their Circumstances, as I have in several Parts of the Company's Records, and this Work, fully demonstrated.

I shall only observe further, that while the Zemindars were at Madras, several Disputes were adjusted amongst them, and they were relieved from what they conceived to be highly injurious and oppressive to them, certain Taxes and Impositions charged by the Company's Dubash Vincaty Royaloo. The whole Proceedings are on the Company's Records, but are not cited by the Secret Committee. When the Zemindars left Madras, they wrote me a Letter of Acknowledgment on the Subject (*p*).

to twelve Lacks of Pagodas, within a Trifle. The Secret Committee state, that, on the 29th February 1780, the Amount of the Balances was something more than seventeen Lacks; which *implies* an Increase of about five Lacks during my Government. But—deducting from this Sum, what was afterwards brought to the Company's Credit, upon closing the Books, in April of the same Year; as also the Amount of the *increase* upon the Tribute which I had stipulated, but which was not collected by the Subordinates, and the Amount of Teeps due;

I am convinced it will appear, that the Balances did *not at all increase* during my Government.—Nay, when it is considered, that of these seventeen Lacks, *upwards of three* were due from the Chicacole Circar; which the President and Council, as well as Mr. Casamajor, admit to be secure; it will surely be allowed, that proper Measures were taken, during my Administration, *for the Reduction of Balances*.

(*p*) See my App. No. 16.

APPENDIX

TO

SIR THOMAS RUMBOLD's

DEFENCE.

LONDON, 1782.

No. I.

Extract of a Letter from Sir Thomas Rumbold, to the Chairman of the Honourable United East-India Company.

Dated Fort St. George, 20th May, 1778.

"I HAVE been under some Difficulty with respect to your Circars, the shameful Scene of Abuse, which has been uniformly committed in your Northern Chiefships, called for our particular Attention. The Advantages you hoped from the Committee of Circuit have not been much felt, I have reflected much on this Subject as being very important to you, and can conceive no Mode so likely to place your Circars upon a firm and proper Footing, as to call the dependant Zemindars to the Presidency, and there settle with them for the different Countries; this Measure evidently breaks through those Chains of little Politics, which have so long subsisted in your Northern Governments, which constantly kept your Troops in the Field upon some pretended Occasion or other, it teaches them to place their Dependance on your Government alone; opens to them the proper Channel for Redress, and fixes a Communication between your Presidency and your most distant Dependants. I intend letting the Lands for a Term of five Years, and the Event will, I flatter myself, prove to the Advantage of the Measure."

No. I.

Extract of a Letter from Sir Thomas Rumbold, to the Chairman of the Honourable East-India Company.

Dated Fort St. George, November 15th, 1778.

"THE heavy Balances that were due and accumulating from the Northern Zemindars, I have no Doubt will now be recovered, and that your Revenue there will be on a more secure Footing than ever. The uncontrouled Power of the Chiefs of the Northern Settlements, and the mutual Interests that subsisted between them and this Government, I am persuaded was very oppressive to the Zemindars, and detrimental both to your Revenue and Commerce. The Alteration that has taken Place by fixing their Jemmabundy here, will be productive of the best Consequences to the Company; tho' it will require Time for the Zemindars to recover from the Load of Debt with which they are burthened, and the utmost Attention and Indulgence must be given to promote the Cultivation of their Lands. The Determination of calling the Zemindars to the Presidency has struck at the Root of those Evils which they complained of, and it is the Subordinate Chiefs alone that will probably wish the Measures we have taken had been dispensed with."

No. I.

Copy of a Letter from Lord Weymouth, one of his Majesty's Secretaries of State.

Dated St. James's, 23d March 1779.

" SIR;

" I Have received your Letter of the 23d October last, and have laid it before the King.

" I have in Command from his Majesty to express to you his Satisfaction at the Conduct of your Presidency in the Execution of the Orders sent from hence for the Reduction of Pondicherry. The considerable Share you have had, Sir, in forwarding this Measure, meets with his Majesty's Approbation, who has been graci-
" ously

" oufly pleafed on this Occafion to confer on you the Dignity of a
" Baronet of Great-Britain.

" I have received his Majefty's Commands with particular Satis-
" faction, and beg Leave to offer you my Congratulations on this
" diftinguifhed Mark of his Majefty's Favour. I am with great
" Truth and Regard,

     Sir,
      Your moft obedient
       humble Servant,

          Weymouth."

No. I.

Extract from the Eaft India Company's general Letter, with the Thanks of the Court of Proprietors, to Sir Thomas Rumbold, Bart.

      Dated London 14th April 1779.

Our Prefident and Council at Fort St. George.

" YOUR Letters by the Cormorant, advifing of the Reduction of
" Pondicherry, were delivered to us by Lieutenant Rumbold,
" the 16th Ult. your Conduct has been very meritorious, that great
" Event is exceedingly important in Point of Time, and of the
" greateft Confequence to this Country. The Honours conferred
" by his Majefty on Sir Thomas Rumbold and Sir Hector Munro,
" are the moft undoubted Proofs of Royal Approbation, and it is
" with the greateft Pleafure we hereby tranfmit the unanimous
" Thanks of a very numerous Court of Proprietors, to our Gover-
" nor, to the Commander in Chief of our Troops, and to the Ad-
" miral and Commander in Chief of his Majefty's Ships in India,
" for the very fignal Services rendered to their Country, and to the
" Eaft India Company, on the late Occafion."

At a General Court of the United Company of Merchants of England trading to the Eaft-Indies, held on Wednefday the 7th April 1779.

          Refolved

Refolved unanimoufly, "That the Thanks of this Court be given to
"Sir Thomas Rumbold, Bart. Prefident of the Council of
"Fort St. George, for the very important Service he has ren-
"dered to the Nation and this Country, by the Zeal and At-
"tention he has manifefted in carrying the Orders of the Secret
"Committee, for commencing Hoftilities into immediate Exe-
"cution."

No. II.

STATE of the BALANCES at Mafulipatam, April 1778.

The Payment in Kifts, from 1ft Dec. 1777, to 1ft May, 1778, to be received from the Zemindars by Bills on the Soucars, ufually affigned in March and April.			Outftanding Balances to be recovered of 1776, which ought to have been paid by the 25th of Sep- tember, 1777.			Total due to the Com- pany, to be col- lected, and which ought to be received in the Courfe of March, April, and May, 1778.		
Pagodas.								
340,171	16	40	204,842	20	20	545,214	—	60

BALANCE due from the prefent and former Renters of Mafulipatam, and the Havellys, to 13th April, 1778.

Prefent Renters.					
Rupees	16,750	—	and Ps.	46,029	30
Former Renters	36,007	3	and Ps.	38,750	—
Rupees	52,757	3	or Ps.	84,779 15,000	30 —
			Brought down	99,779 545,214	60
Total Balances due from the Diftrict of Mafulipatam				644,993	60

No. II.

No. II.

Extract of a Letter from Anthony Sadlier to Sir Thomas Rumbold.

Dated Mafulipatam, 5th May, 1778.

"THE Rapacity and Peculation of Men, has nearly ruined this Country.—The Misfortunes it is now involved in originates from fuch Principles, and its Effects may have brought on Diftreffes poffibly not to be reformed."

Extracts of a Letter from Anthony Sadlier to Sir Thomas Rumbold.

Dated Mafulipatam, 5th May, 1778.

I. "THE Zemindars have now confented to proceed to Madras, in Confequence of the Order fent them, enforced by us, with every Mark of Submiffion and Obedience becoming our Station, after giving the Subject, referred to you, its due Confideration, and fatisfying yourfelf how the Calls on us for Money here are to be fupplied, I humbly think no Time fhould be loft in compelling the Zemindars Attendance at the Prefidency, that you fhould even fix a Day for their Departure, and empower us here to enforce it with Sepoys. The apparent Violence of fuch a Meafure ought not to deter you, as it commonly requires fuch an Exertion to get them from their refpective Countries here, and when here frequently in Ufe, to attain the Ends of Government in fulfilling their Engagements."

II. "It becomes an Object of your moft ferious Attention, in cafe the Zemindars proceed as at prefent intended, to find Means by which our Treafury may be fupplied. The moft valuable Part of the Company's Inveftment depends on it; and the Zemindars withholding as they do, Affiftance of any Kind, leaves little Hopes of Refources in ourfelves.—For whatever may appear due, fuch is the State of Credit, and fuch the Uncertainty of Payment, I do not at this Hour know where I can apply with certainty for the

" smallest Sums. And all I expect to be able to do will barely furnish
" the Demands of the present Month."

III. " If too, by improper Management heretofore, Deficiency in
" Payment of the Kists now due, and the Revenue of this Country,
" according to its present Settlement should happen,—may not the
" Cause by its Effect of giving the first Shock to common and long
" practised Credit in the Mode, of Security in these Countries, be
" also ascribed to the present Plan? In short, if it happens that the
" Settlement, by bad Seasons and Causes alledged by the Zemindars
" is on the Decline;—would it not be prudent to leave the Govern-
" ment charged hitherto with full Responsibility to justify its,
" Measures, to work out its own Misfortunes, and bear the Censure.
" it deserves?—Are Questions with Deference I submit to your better
." Judgment."

No. III.

Translation of a Letter from Mirzah Rajah Vizeram Rauze, Bahan-
def Mouna Sultan, of his own Hand-writing, to the President and
Governor and Council of Fort St. George.

Dated 4th August, 1777.

" ALTHOUGH we have since the Time of our Ancestors very
" much gained the Company's Favour, and behaved well to-
" wards them, Mr. Johnson, on Account of some Disgust against us,
" has used several Means, and wrote to the Company in order to
" bring us under a blame, and you believed the same to be true,
" therefore we determined ourselves to come there, and declare our
" Truth, but we found Mr. Johnson will never let us go there, on
" Account of which, I have now sent my Brother to you; what-
" ever he speaks to you, you will hear, and take in the same Manner
" as if I likewise was present; and at the same Time you will be
" pleased

"pleased to send an Order to the Chief and Council at Vizagapa-
"tam, for me to come to you: please to look upon this as if it
"was an hundred Letters."

No. III.

Translation of a Letter from Vizeram Rauze to Samuel Johnson,
Esq; (see Appendix No. 16, 2d Report.)

Dated 23d August 1777.

"YOU sent a Letter from the Governor to me by the Hands
" of your Chubdar at Eight o'Clock this Night. I must ac-
" knowledge the Receipt thereof. The Purport of that Letter is,
" that immediately on Receipt of it, to suffer the Company's Troops
" to take Post in the Fort Vizianagrum, and for me to proceed to
" the Presidency, to apply to the Chief and Council for Sepoys to
" escort me thither, and that they will comply with my Request,
" should I delay obeying the Orders, I may probably incur their
" Censure, thereof I request you will on Receipt hereof give the
" necessary Orders for the Troops to be stationed at Vizianagrum,
" and likewise to let me have a Company of Sepoys, to accompany
" me in my Journey to Madras, and to grant me Permission this
" very Day to leave this Place: upon Receipt of which both I, and
" my Brother, will set out for Madras. To delay my Request, will
" be the Means of drawing upon me their severe Displeasure; there-
" fore I repeat my Request, that you will be pleased to comply
" therewith this very Day. *This Letter is meant by me to the Chief
" and Council.* I have replied to the Governor's Letter, and inclosed
" a Copy hereof. The above I write for your Information."

No. IV.

No. IV.

Extract of a Letter from Edward Cotsford to the Honourable the Court of Directors of the United East-India Company.

Dated New-Bond-Street, January 13, 1777.

"ANUNDAH Rauze died in 1759, and leaving no Children, Chundrama (Widow of Vizeram Rauze, who was killed at Bobily) having a great Authority in the Country, and at the Soubah's Court(a), caused the Son of one Rambardrah Rauze who was descended from a collateral Branch of the Family to succeed Anundah Rauze. He was named Vencattyputty, but she, in Memory of her Husband, caused him to be called Vizeram Rauze. This Man(b) is now Zemindar of Vizianagur, Sitteram Rauze in whom all the Power is lodged, is his half Brother (having the same Father) and also older(c), and judging he had the best Claim to the Country, he caused a great deal of Trouble for the Space of a Year, when the Matter was compromised; he giving up the Title to Vizeram Rauze, provided the Management of the Country might be left with him as his Deputy."

No. IV.

Account of the Vizanagrum Family, as obtained by the Enquiries of Sir Thomas Rumbold.

CHUNDERAMAH, was the Widow of Vizeram Rauze, from his superior Abilities, stiled, The Great, and was the Rajah of Vizianagrum; he had no Children, but appointed his Cousin Annunde Guzzapetty Rauze to succeed to his Zemindary; and Chunderamah had sufficient Interest with her Husband to persuade him to take her favourite Nephew the present Vizeram Rauze into her House, to educate him, and to adopt him to succeed to the Rajahship, in Case of the Death of Annunde Guzzapetty Rauze. The latter died
of

(a) Hydrabad. (b) He is about 29 Years of Age. (c) He is about 36 Years of Age.

of the Small-Pox at Rajahmundry; and Chunderamah, after the decease of her Husband, being a Woman of great Abilities, and general good Character, drew the Respect and Attention of all Degrees of People in the Districts, and had sufficient Interest to get the present Vizeram Rauze appointed, agreeable to the Adoption of her late Husband, and to satisfy the elder Brother Sitteram Rauze, who attempted to frustrate her Views, the Management of the Country was given to him, whilst Vizeram Rauze was only to retain the Rank and State attendant on the Rajahship. The Brothers were the Nephews of Chunderamah. Sitteram Rauze is the Elder by a lawful Marriage, and had Hereditary Succession taken Place would have been intitled to the Zemindary in Preference to his Brother, who was by a second Marriage.

No. V.

Heads of the Conference of Rajah Vizeram Rauze, in the Presence of Lieutenant Fowke and Swammy Dubash, to Colonel Braithwaite and one of the Rajah's own People

"THE Rajah comes to Colonel Braithwaite in the deepest Concern, he fears that Mr. Johnson and the Council are angry: he understands they meant to confine Setteram Rauze, his Brother, within the Fort, this has been publickly talked of, and prevents his Brother paying that Visit which he acknowledges he ought to do. He confesses to have written to the Council against his Brother: he is sensible of the ready Assistance given in the Manner of bringing down his Brother. He is sensible of the Chief and Council's Goodness in forgiving all Things and becoming Friends; he thanks Colonel Braithwaite for being the Mediator; he entreats he will again undertake that Office; he is ready and willing to comply with all their Desires; he will submit to all Things; his Fort is small, his House, his Family, his Women are in it, they know this; it is not an offensive Fort; it is a common Eastern Defence round the Palace. Nevertheless, in regard

"to that, he will obey the Company's Orders, if they are positively
"determined to garrison it, he trusts the Chief and Council will
"represent this favourably at Madras, and wait Orders from thence;
"he knows their Goodness, he has but one Favour to ask, and he
"will ask it in any Manner they think proper; that they will not
"bring eternal Disgrace upon him by making his Brother a Pri-
"soner. It never was nor could be his Intentions that such a Dis-
"grace should fall upon his Family; he applied for his Brother to
"settle Accounts; he shall settle them, he shall pay every Farthing;
"the Gentlemen shall be satisfied that he does; he believes his Bro-
"ther's Heart is humbled by this late Quarrel with the Company;
"whether it is, or is not, he will never listen to his Advice. If
"the Gentlemen have written to Madras about his Brother, he will
"be answerable for his Brother; the Gentlemen may mount a
"Guard upon his Brother in the Tope, or they may send him to
"Madras under an Escort; but to confine him here in his Presence
"on his Account, he cannot live to see it, his God will not permit it;
"he entreats this severe Disgrace may not be thought on; he re-
"quests that his Brother's Son and Daughter, Wife, and his Mo-
"ther-in-Law, may be allowed to retire to Vizianagrum; he will
"be answerable to pay all Demands; he concludes with Tears in
"his Eyes, with a solemn Declaration, that he and all his People
"are determined to die, if this harsh Measure in Regard to his Bro-
"ther must have Way; he will not oppose the Company, he will
"not die fighting; he will not draw innocent People into a Scrape;
"they will die quietly by their own Weapons."

The Original of the Above is in Sir Thomas Rumbold's Possession, attested and signed by Lieutenant Fowke, the Persian Interpreter to Colonel Braithwaite.

No. V.

Colonel Braithwaite's Letter respecting Setteram Rauze.

"COLONEL Braithwaite never was an Advocate for Setteram
" Rauze, he arrived a Stranger in this District; the only Persons
"from whom he could receive any Accounts or Information, were
"from a Man averse to Setteram, all he heard of him was bad, from
" Jaggernaut

" Jaggernaut Rauze, as also from Mr. Johnson, in private Conver-
" sation, he understood that Setteram Rauze was going to make his
" Escape, with all his Brother's Treasure, and Jewels, this was also
" confirmed by an Hircarrah, but this Hircarrah was also in the In-
" terest of Jaggernaut Rauze. Mr. Johnson wanted Setteram to be
" seized at any Rate; it could not be done without an Order from
" the Board, and Jaggernaut Rauze prevailed on the Rajah to write
" into the Board a Complaint against Setteram. A Detachment was
" sent to bring him; after it was gone, the Colonel called to Mind,
" that the Presidency had positively forbid the Commencement of
" any Hostilities, till their further Orders; he conceived this either
" was in itself, or would produce some Act of Hostility. He called
" Mr. Johnson up in the Night, and recommended that he might
" send another Officer, with a Letter and fair Words to Setteram
" Rauze, advising him, for his own Good, to come down, on the
" Colonel's Parole, to Vizagapatam, and to deliver the Gate of An-
" capilly, in which it was supposed all the Treasure he had stolen
" was lodged; this he chearfully submitted to; Lieutenant Colonel
" Nelson took Possession of the Gate, and placed Centinels all around,
" so that nothing could escape from the Place, and Setteram came to
" Vizagapatam upon the Colonel's Parole, authorised by the Chief
" and Council of Vizagapatam. The Rajah wrote to contradict every
" Thing about his Brother, and repeatedly declared to the Colonel
" that all Accounts were clear; that he had no Charge against his
" Brother; that he had been wrought upon to do what he had done;
" of this Lieutenant Fowke, who was Interpreter, is Witness. Mr.
" Johnson wanted to have Setteram a Prisoner in the Fort; the Rajah
" opposed this, declaring that he would die, and all his People by
" their own Hands, if that was done. The Colonel opposed it, on
" Account of the Parole given; the Rajah's Declaration was given
" in Form to Mr. Johnson; the Point was given up, and Setteram
" remained with his Brother, and so far from giving him bad Ad-
" vice, it should appear he gave him good, for the Rajah in every
" Thing conformed to the Orders of the Presidency. Setteram Rauze
" (altho' tainted with a very bad Character) in every Thing which
" the Colonel had to do with him, gave not the smallest Offence to
" the Company, and rather deserves Praise than Blame, from the
" Æra the Colonel speaks of; as to former Transactions the Colonel
" knows nothing of them positively; the Reports he heard were
" against Setteram; as a Servant of the Company he had no one
                                                      " Fault

" Fault to lay to his Charge. The Devil ought to have his Due, and
" the Colonel has intended no further. As his Letters on Records
" to the Chief and Council of Vizagapatam, and their Anſwers will
" ſhew,—which cannot, he preſumes, be deſtroyed, and he thinks
" ought to be now before the Preſidency."

No. VI.

Extract of a Letter from the Chief and Council of Vizagapatam to the Governor and Council at Fort St. George.

Dated 24th Dec., 1777.

Appendix, No. 23, 2d Report.

HIS (Vizeram Rauze) great Debt to Individuals, which he is incapable of paying off, or any Part thereof, from his Loſs of Credit with the Soucars, who have in general entertained a Notion that the Honourable Board will never reſtore him to his antient Reſidence, and of Courſe are apprehenſive his Affairs are in ſuch a Predicament as will involve him in Difficulties that he cannot extricate himſelf from. He is full of Fears and Apprehenſions, that during his Abſence all the Hill People will deſtroy his Country, which he at preſent keeps in ſome Order, by Negociation with ſome of their Head Men, or Chiefs. He is wherewithal ſo ſuperſtitious, which is the Characteriſtick of the Gentoos, that he is led to think it will be impoſſible to recover his ancient Family Habitation, without he is continually employed in Supplication to his Deity, for the Company's Favour and Protection; for which Purpoſe he is encamped near the Pagoda, on the Hill of Sumachilum, and means not, as it is reported, to quit it before your Honour, &c. reſtore to him his Fort of Vizianagrum; which Circumſtance, altho' founded in Ignorance and Superſtition, we hope will merit ſome Degree of Attention from the Honourable Board.

No. VI.

Copy of a Letter from Archibald Eagle, Lieutenant Commander of the five Companies of Rajah's Sibbendy, to Sir Thomas Rumbold, Baronet, Prefident and Governor of Fort St. George.

Dated Fort St. George, 30th March, 1780.

SIR,

I Have the Honour to receive your Commands to lay before you a State of the Fort of Vizianagrum.

I left that Country on Account of bad Health about the Middle of laft September, and fhall defcribe the Fort and its particular Situation at that Time. It is diftant about thirty Miles from Vizagapatam, (running nine in Land) and fomewhat farther from Chicacole, but nearly centrical between both. The Fort is of an oblong Form, about half a Mile in Circumference, furrounded by a Wall and dry Ditch. The Houfe and Garden of the Rajah poffefs the principal Part, the remaining Space is occupied by his Family and Domeftics. The Country People live in the Pittah, which comes clofe to the Brink of the Ditch. The Fort is overlooked by an Eminence within Gun-fhot, which commands it in every Part: And parallel to one Face runs a very thick Bank of a Tunk about half the Height of the Walls, and within an hundred Yards. It has not the Advantage of a Glacis, or any kind of Outwork, and is fo deftitute of the Means of Defence, that it can only be confidered as a Place of Safety to the Perfon of the Rajah againft the Hill Polygars, who frequently come down in great Numbers, and commit every Sort of Depredation. The Walls are of unhewn Stone laid in Mud, and fo far from being able to refift the Shock of battering Cannon, I am confident that the Fire of Field Pieces would make a practicable Breach in a few Hours: One Face is cafed with Brick and Chunam, but in a very decayed State, and on another is a Breach capable of admitting a Company of Sepoys a-breaft. There are Cracks in fo many Places, that a Row of half-fized Gabions filled with Earth has been placed along the Top to prevent the Impreffions of the Weather; and were it not for this Precaution, it is my Opinion the Walls of Vizianagrum could not withstand the Rains of a severe Monsoon.

Upon the whole, I am humbly of Opinion, that under the Circumstances already set forth, the circumscribed Dimensions—totally unfurnished with Bomb Proofs, and having only one small Magazine, the Fort of Vizianagrum would not be a safe Lodgment for Troops and Military Stores, should a respectable Enemy appear in that Part of the Country.

I have the Honour to subscribe myself with much Respect,
                                Sir,
Fort St. George,   Your most obedient,
30th March 1780.   humble Servant,
                                        Arch. Eagle,
    Commander of the five Companies of Rajah's Sibbendy.

No. VI.

Extract of a Letter from the Committee of Circuit to the President and Governor, &c. Council of Fort St. George.

Dated 27th August, 1777.

" WITH Respect to the Forts, we are of Opinion that it may be
"   proper to bring the Rajah to deliver up that of Vizianagrum;
" not that we suppose he depends upon it as a Place of Defence, but
" we believe he is greatly attached to it on Account of the Length of
" Time his Family has resided there; that he will probably be afraid,
" on Account of his Women, of continuing there when it is gar-
" risoned by our Troops, and will dread the Mortification and
" Disgrace of being obliged to remove. It is a small Fort about
" 200 Yards square, with a dry unfinished Ditch, and has four round
" Bastions at the Angles; the Body of the Fort is at present in pretty
" good Repair, and is partly of Brick and partly of Stone, cemented
" on the Outside with Chunam. By the Construction of it, which
" is wholly in the Country Stile of fortifying, without any Out-
" works, we conceive that it cannot be deemed strong. There are
                                                    " but

" but few Buildings in it, confifting of the Rajah's Dwelling-Houfe
" with the Outhoufes, a fmall Bomb Proof, and fome Sheds for the
" Rajah's People. We do not imagine it to be a Place of any Con-
" fequence, confidered as a Fortification; but the leaving it in the
" Rajah's Hands, might make other Zemindars expect the fame In-
" dulgences. We fhould think it more advifeable to allow the
" Rajah an Addition to his Guard than the Poffeffion of his Fort;
" and rather the Poffeffion of his Fort, than that the infifting on this
" Article alone fhould be the Occafion of a total Breach with him.—
" His holding the Fort cannot put it in his Power ever hereafter to
" do us Mifchief:—And in order to effect quietly a great Change,
" all immaterial or unimportant Matters fhould, we think, be
" facrificed."

Extract of a Letter from James Henry Cafamajor, Chief of Vizagapatam, to Sir Thomas Rumbold.

Dated Vizagapatam, 20th December, 1780.

" AS I have taken up this Ground, I beg Leave to exercife your
" Patience a little longer, by informing you of the Situation
" of public Matters in this Circar, and I am the more inclined to do
" fo, becaufe I conceive you will derive Satisfaction from the Re-
" lation, being connected with the Subject as one of the principal
" Tranfactions of your Government.—On my Arrival here, I found
" the Province loaded with an Arrear to the Company, amounting
" altogether to Fourteen Lacks of Rupees, of which upwards of
" Twelve Lacks were due from the Vizianagrum Family for Jem-
" mabundy, and Havelly Rents, &c. Setteram Rauze, *on whom all*
" *depended*, did not return from Madras until the 8th of October:
" When he arrived at the Capital his Meffengers, in his Abfence,
" always wanted to refer Matters to their Mafter to gain Time.
" Thus circumftanced, and the Refponfibility with which I con-
" fidered myfelf invefted from my Station, induced me to adopt,
" without Referve, the Refolution of interfering by a certain Day,
" in the Collections, on the Part of the Company; but before the
" fixed Period arrived, I found an Alteration produced, which ren-
" dered fuch a Step unneceffary;—Money was paid faft into the
" Treafury.—On Sitteram Rauze's Arrival, I gave him to under-
" ftand,

" stand, what I conceived to be the Line he ought to adopt with Re-
" gard to his Duties connected with this Government; and that I
" did not tell it as a Matter of Opinion only, but that it must be
" attended to without Reserve or Evasion.—He saw the Necessity of
" following my Advice; and this Conduct has enabled me to dis-
" charge my public Trust with some Degree of Satisfaction, and it
" has met with the Approbation of the Presidency. I have been
" able to remit from the Collections to the Treasury of the Presi-
" dency 120,000 Rupees; I have in Readiness to send by the very
" first Opportunity 200,000 Rupees.—I have already advanced for
" the Investment 160,000, and the Issues made for general Disburse-
" ments from my Arrival to this Period amounts to 200,000
" Rupees; so except about 60,000 Rupees which I found in the
" Chest on my Arrival, the Remainder amounting to 620,000 Ru-
" pees, has been collected from the Time I took Charge of this
" Office; and I have the best Hope from the Arrangements made,
" to be able to send a further Supply of 250,000 Rupees at least to
" the Presidency by May, exclusive of the Two Lacks ready for that
" Purpose, and the 120,000 Rupees actually forwarded; and by the
" 20th of April next, there will arise Expences at this Place, which
" will amount to about 200,000 Rupees for general Disbursements,
" Provisions for Madras, and some Advances to keep the Weavers
" from starving; all which I shall be able to discharge from the
" Collections. And this exists not in Idea only, the greater Part
" you will see has been accomplished; and I have almost a moral
" Certainty of fulfilling the rest, if this District continues in Peace.
" And then I shall have the Satisfaction to reflect, that from the
" Transactions of my first Year's Residence here, you will have no
" Reason to reproach yourself for having done me the Favour to
" interest yourself in my Appointment. I have, besides, since my
" Arrival, dispatched 500 Bales, worth about 120,000 Rupees:
" And by the End of next Month 500 Bales more will be sent to
" the Presidency, being mostly the Produce of the Money advanced in
" my Time: And it may not be improper to remark, by Way of
" Conclusion, that for many Years past, this Subordinate never
" made Remittances of Cash; on the contrary, it received Supplies
" for its Investment.—Sitteram Rauze is on a good Footing with his
" Brother, but as he finds he has many Enemies, he intends to live
" at Vizagapatam with his Family, during these Times of public
" Distress."

No. VII.

No. VII.

Debts due from the following Zemindars to Individuals, as given in by themselves.

Rajah Jaggaputty Rauze, till 26th September 1778.

GOVURDAN Dofs and Virjey Dofs	55,328
Verjey Dofs	51,828
Chuckra Huvdanlah Lutcheme Nurfinva Cheanloo	11,400
Mr. Pringle	10,000
Doctor Singular	7,300
Mr. Davidfon	450
Ragava Rauze	13,000
Mondaloo Puddue	6,000
Ms. Pagodas	155,306

Culdindu Tupputty Rauze, till 26th September 1778.

Govurdan Dofs	200,000
Verjey Dofs	8,000
Chuckra Huvdanla Lutcheme Nurfinva Cheanloo	30,000
Suncaramunjey Vofsdeva Charloo	12,000
Mr. James Hodges	25,000
Mr. Alexander Jamefon	3,000
Doctor Singular	2,250
In fmall Sums to different Perfons	10,000
Ms. Pagodas	290,250

F Reddy

Reddy Lutcheme Narrain Doo, till 25th September 1778.

Govurdan Dofs and Verjey Dofs	2,150
Verjey Dofs	7,400
Dauzeny Iijapah	1,800
Mondatoo Gopunnah	1,400
Chuckra Huvdanla Lutcheme Nurfinva Cheanuloo	2,540
Cunjemurty Vincatachellam	820
Ms. Pagodas	16,110

Conatty Nurfinvaloo, till 24 September 1778.

Vincatafa Norjadoo	2,000
Daufery Gruva Chilly	2,842
Yanuga Sumpudoo	528
Punta Sittaramudoo	630
Ms. Pagodas	6,000

Riddy Mungaputty Doo, till 25 September 1778.

Govurdana Dofs	2,000
Verjey Dofs	6,500
Chuckra Huvdanla Nurfinva Cheanuloo	2,350
Jondyconda Vincataroyaloo	1,800
Mondatoo Gopunnah	1,150
Ms. Pagodas	13,800

Mondapauty Tripputty Rauze, till 24th September 1778.

Daumodara Dofs	6,287
Lal Dofs and Verjey Dofs	2,000
Dovva Nuttoojey Caufey Dofs	1,000
Uzey Dofloo	1,000
Daufery Gruva Chitty	2,000
Mondatoo Gopunnah	2,000
Mondrapacada Vencatramanah	1,000
Prayagah Bampanah	500
Bommagunder Joakey	600
Buyapafitty Royaloo	600
Yetta Vencatachellam	560
Ms. Pagodas	17,547

Mecca Opparow, till 26th September 1778.

Mr. Hodges	31,504
Mr. Pringle	28,307
Captain Lyfaught	3,700
Lieutenant Towns	8,183
Condraigula Vencatarow	19,000
Soucars at Mafulipatam	184,116¼
Madras Pagodas	274,810¼

Caucir-

Caucirlamoody Vencataputty Rauze, till 24 September 1778.

Lal Dofs	24,650
Govurdan Dofs	3,000
Dovva Nuttoojey Caufey Dofs	1,000
Jaggaputty Rauze	8,000
Chuckra Huvdanla Lutcheme Nurfinva Cheanluloo	1,000
Rajah Ram Naig	1,000
Dontaloor Butchamah	2,500
Mondaty Puddue	1,000
Gruva Chitty	1,000
Cunjemurty Vencatachellam	2,000
Colloony Ramudoo	600
Dontaloor Triputty Rauze	1,000
Jumpana Vizia Jagganada Rauze	1,000
Canucurty Chundrapah	500
Irevengadom	500
Mr. Hodges	1,600
Monf. Berry	500
Madras Pagodas	50,850

No. VII.

An Account of Money owing by the Zemindars in the Mafulipatam Diftrict to Soucars and other Individuals, tranfmitted by Mr. Sadlier to Sir Thomas Rumbold.

Ragonaut Naik, Soucar, Gomaftah of Goverden Dofs of Hydrabaud, his Account with Culdindee Trippetterauze, now owing	183,900
Vaffereddy Raumaunah	40,100
Carried over Ps.	224,000

Macca

Brought over	224,000
Macca Narſinva Opporow	6,300
Sooranany Narſinvarow and Vecataramrow	1,800
Mundapatty Tripitterauze	282
Vachavoy Juggapetterauze	5,000
Jogue Rauze	1,150
Cacarlamoody Ramachandre Rauze	2,500
Peree Charla Rajanah	4,500
Latchmee Nairamdoo and Munga Puddoo	6,500
Veeraſha Lingum	1,600
Cotar Letchimy Doſs Soucar, his Account with Macca Narſinva Opparow	3,000
Collavacollue Timmanarow	3,000
Collavacollue Timmanarow and Chinna Row	15,400
Varugonda Rammanah	15,000
Vellunky Gopaul Row, and Vencaty Row	500
Vellunky Mullarow	4,000
Sooranany Narſinvarow and Vencataramrow	23,500
Sooranany Vencatarow	5,900
Verjee Doſs Soucar, his Account with Macca Narſinva Opparow	163,400
Row Mahepellerow	17,900
Voſſareddy Ramanah	7,700
Sooranany Narſinvarow	1,199
Jewpallee Narſinvarow	10,400
Cacarlamoody Ramachandrerauze	8,000
Cacarlamoody Vencatapellerauze of Cotta	30,000
Mundapatty Trippetterauze	5,200
Kiſſarah Sooranah Deſmook	1,500
Collavacollue Timmanarow	600
Codant Ram	30,500
Total Amount, Pagodas	600:331

G

No. VIII.

Extract of a Letter from Mr. Cotsford, Chief and Council, to Sir Thomas Rumbold, Baronet, President and Governor, &c. Fort St. George.

Dated Masulipatam, 23d March, 1780.

"HAVING replied to the several Paragraphs of your above Letter, we proceed to notice what has passed on the Subject of Revenue, since the Date of our last. We have the Satisfaction to acquaint your Honour, &c. that the following Zemindars have given in Teeps for the three Kists due in September, viz. Jaggaputty Rauze, of Peddapore, to the Amount of Madras Pagodas 42,657 : 9.—Trippetty Rauze, of Muggletore, for his own Zemindary, and Security, Country Pagodas 85,636 : 15 : 60. Ramchunderauze, to the Amount of 3,913 : 6 : 60. Codant Ram of Sallapillu, has paid in six Kists, on Account of Phazelly 1189, or 1780, so that no further Payments are due from him until the Month of September; we conceive it our Duty to Notice to your Honour, &c. the punctual Payment of this Zemindar, which at a Time when most of the other Tributaries continue so much in Arrears, appears to us particularly commendable.

"Vassreddy Ramana of Nandigamah has paid six Kists in full for Phazelly 1188 or 1779.

"All the Zemindars and other Tributaries of these Districts, as well those above-mentioned, as others, whom we have not had Occasion to notice in this Letter, are either arrived, or will shortly be here, to adjust the Business of their further Payments. And we beg Leave to assure your Honour, &c. that our utmost Endeavours shall be exerted towards accomplishing the Object of your late repeated Orders, viz. the obtaining from them not only Payment of their annual Tribute, but such Part of their Arrears as may be due at this Period. We see the Necessity upon this Occasion, for the vigorous Exertion of the Powers you have lodged
"with

" with us, in the ſtrongeſt Point of View; being fully perſuaded,
" that if we ſhould fail at this Time, in the Execution of your
" Orders, the beſt Opportunity for accompliſhing them will thereby
" certainly be loſt; and the Recovery of a conſiderable Part, if not
" the Whole of the Arrears become hereafter very dubious. The
" Zemindars Trepetty Rauze, and Jaggapetty Rauze, have been re-
" markably ſlow in their Payments, during the Courſe of the laſt
" Year; nor could we procure theſe Payments at all without a De-
" gree of Compulſion: This Refractorineſs of Conduct, when they
" had but a ſmall Sum to make good, compared to the Demand now
" upon them, appears to us a reaſonable Ground of Suſpicion, they
" will try every Art and Method to delay their Payments at this
" Time; we have therefore come to the Reſolution of recommending
" to the Chief, that after having diſcuſſed the Buſineſs for which
" they are now called down, and aſſured them of every Indulgence
" your Orders will permit us to ſhew them, if he finds that it has not
" the proper Effect, he proceed to acquaint them, that your Orders
" are ſo poſitive for procuring the Payments, they will not be ſuffered
" to ſtir from this Place until they have complied with them. We
" have indeed little Expectation of ſucceeding with theſe Zemindars,
" unleſs they are previouſly convinced that they will be proceeded
" againſt to Extremity, in Caſe of Non-compliance; but at the ſame
" Time, we are not leſs of Opinion, that if the Meaſures we mean
" to purſue, receive your Approbation and Support, the Whole of
" what is due at this Period, not only from theſe laſt Zemindars,
" but from *all* the Tributaries of this Diſtrict will be obtained from
" them."

No. VIII.

Extract of a Letter from Mr. Cotsford, Chief of Maſulipatam, to Sir Thomas Rumbold, Governor of Fort St. George.

Dated 19th Auguſt 1779.

" I Am glad the Buſineſs of the Farms is decided, and perfectly
"   ſatisfied with the Manner in which it is done. The Syſtem of
" Management ſo far as our preſent Experience can enable us to
"   " judge

" judge of it, appears to me to have been a losing one, and in
" Speculation it seems to have been the worst that could have been
" adopted. I was some Days ago on the Point of writing to you,
" to apprize you of the Inconveniences that were to be apprehended
" from any further Delay in this Matter of the Farms; but hearing
" that it was purely the Consequence of your ill State of Health,
" and that we might expect to hear of the Disposal of the Farms, at
" least in a few Days, I laid aside the Intention as unnecessary."

II. I have been waiting for some Days past for the Account with our Soucars, that I might furnish you with a Statement of what we had received, and what remains due from them of the six Kists given in by the different Zemindars. I have at length got it from them; the Amount of all the Kists paid in Madras Pagodas 366,736 : 30 : 20. That of the Sums received upon all of them is Madras Pagodas 165,014 : 11 : 20, and consequently what remains due (of which we may expect Payment within a short Time) Madras Pagodas 201,722 : 9. This is all we have to depend upon until the Time arrives for settling with them next Year.

III. The greater Part of the Zemindars have given in Petitions for an Indulgence of four Years to discharge their Balances, which we think is as little Time as can be allowed them.. There are two of them however, concerning whom I have in a Minute relating to these Matters expressed an Opinion that their Circumstances "might
" perhaps enable them to pay off what they owe in a shorter Time,
" Codant Ram, of Sallapillee, and Mundapatty Tripute Rauze, or
" Corecundah. The former has the Reputation of being very clear
" and unincumbered in his Affairs by good Management of them;
" the latter is said to be rated very low in Proportion to his Rents,
" in the Jemmabundy Lift. But I have introduced it merely as a
" Conjecture; and very probably with respect to the former, you
" may think it better Policy as tending to recommend and encou-
" rage Oeconomy and good Husbandry, to favour Codant Ram in
" the same Manner with the rest, than to appear in the last to
" check it by partial Rigidness."

IV. " Juggaputty Rauze gave his Teep for six Kists on the 31st of
" July, and we are now proceeding in the Business of recovering
" the Debt due to him by Mahaputty Row."

No. IX.

No. IX.

The following Note was furnished me by a Gentleman perfectly acquainted with the Business in the Ganjam District.

THE Collections for the last four or five Years preceding the Commencement of Ball Kistnah's Term, viz. from September 1774 to September 1779, do not Amount one Year with another to what Ball Kistnah has agreed to give by many thousand Rupees. This is a Truth that the Company's Books now in the India-House will put beyond a Doubt; the same Books will also shew that the making the Collections for the five Years above-mentioned was attended with very heavy Expences, and that the Military and Civil Charges of Ganjam, the Military and Civil Stores sent there from Madras annually, and the Assistance of Troops from Vizagapatam swallowed up the greatest Part of the Collections. It is true some Money has been sent from Ganjam to Madras, and to Vizagapatam at different Times, but when the Charges of Troops from the latter, and the Amount of Civil Stores for Use and Sale, and Military Stores annually sent from the former, and other Charges at Madras, Account Ganjam are placed against the Money received from that Place, the clear annual Profit to the Company from the Ganjam District will be found to have been very trifling. Whereas, as that Country is now settled under Ball Kistnah, there is not a Doubt but a very great annual Profit will accrue to the Company from it.

Ball Kistnah is to pay the Company, *per Annum*, Rs. 455,000
The Sea and River Customs not let to him   -   12,000

Brings the Ganjam Revenue to Rs.   - -   467,000

Which is many thousand Rupees a Year more than the Company received for the last five Years, and this Revenue is not subject to Diminution by Charges of Collection, as Ball Kistnah has agreed to pay these Charges, but 467,000 Rupees is to come into the Company's Cash clear of all Charges, except when any Zemindar refuses to pay his just Jammabundy, and then the Company are to be at the Expence of compelling him.

Ball Kiftna has been upwards of 10 Years the Company's principal native Servant at Ganjam, is perfonally known to all the Zemindars and People of all Degrees in the Ganjam Diftrict, underftands their Language, and knows the Characters, Difpofitions, Countries, and Refources of every one of them, is reckoned a fenfible Man, and the Zemindars have all great Deference for his Judgment, and from his long Experience is very converfant in Revenue Bufinefs, his own Intereft; that powerful incentive will lead him moft heartily to Endeavour to keep the Zemindars and Renters punctual in their Payments, and fteady in the Obfervance of a proper Conduct, fo as to prevent the Neceflity of Military Expeditions againft the Zemindars, which have been the Deftruction of the Ganjam Revenue for many Years, and which Expeditions muft terminate as much to his (the Renter's) as to the Company's Detriment. Hence there may be prefumed a much greater Probability of that Country being free of Difturbances from Ball Kiftnah's collecting the Revenues, refponfible as he is for them, than if they are collected by a Chief and Council, without any fuch intermediate refponfible Officer. Ganjam is a hilly woody Country, in which there are many ftrong Holds, favourable for Refiftance to the Company's Authority. Eleven Years Experience has fhewn the Company that this Country is very difficult to manage to Advantage. The Chief and Council, from their Ignorance of the Country Language, muft rely on Information from native Servants, where Inclination and Intereft may fometime be to magnify and mifreprefent the Conduct of Zemindars, and thereby put the Company to Military Expences, that perhaps were unneceflary, and might have been avoided if the Chiefs and Council underftood the Language of the Country. Every Chief has generally a private Servant, in whom he often puts more Confidence than in the Company's public Head native Servant, and from Cuftom of the Service, all Correfpondence and Converfations with the Zemindars being moftly carried on by the Chief. His is the only public Channel of Information to the Council; hence if the native Servants have the Chief's Ear, and a Mind to mifreprefent Things to him, it is difficult for the Council to find out the true Situation of Matters; the many Difadvantages Gentlemen labour under, particularly in the Ganjam Diftrict, from a Want of Knowledge in the Country Language, are fuch, that I am clearly of Opinion, they cannot manage the Revenue fo well by native Servants, as they can do it through one, who is refponfible for the Revenue,

and

and whofe Intereft it is to keep the Country in Peace, and who is capable of doing it if any one is.

The Poverty of the Ganjam Zemindars, and their Incapacity to pay their former Jemmabundy, has been written from Ganjam to Madras; and thefe Letters, many of them, figned by Mr. Smith. The Prefident, in one of his Minutes, reprefented that there was a Neceffity for eftablifhing a new Jemmabundy through the Ganjam Diftrict, whether the Country was rented or managed by the Chief and Council; it was in confequence brought on the Carpet. Mr. Smith, in his Minute N° 61, in the Appendix 2d Report (fpeaking of the fix Mahindra Mulles Zemindaries) fays, that though their Jemmabundy was 55,000 Rupees *per Annum*, the Medium Collections for nine Years were only 19,000 Rupees *per Annum*. The Ganjam Gentlemen fay (vide N° 33 in the Appendix, 2d Report) that five of the moft capital Zemindars are fcarcely able to maintain their Families with common Decency; and that the heavy Balances of the Moherry Zemindary arofe from an over-rated Jemmabundy.

Ball Kiftnah confented to and propofed that the Jemmabundy fhould be leffened 78,000 Rupees a Year, knowing that Sum had never been and never could be collected.

Ball Kiftnah, by his Agreement with the Company, is authorized to collect from the feveral Zemindars a Jemmabundy of 308,700 Rupees: Their Jemmabundy before was called 386,000 Rupees, as will appear by the Appendix N° 62, 2d Report, fo that his Collections will be lefs than the former nominal Jemmabundy by 78,000 Rupees *per Annum*.

The former Jemmabundy for the Zemindary's Havelly Lands, Sea Cuftoms, &c. was called	Rupees 555,000
Deduct fo much as it is reduced	78,000
And there remains	Rupees 477,000
There muft alfo be deducted the Sea Cuftoms, which are not let to Ball Kiftnah	12,000
	Rupees 465,000

This

This Sum of 465,000 Rupees is all that Ball Kiftnah is allowed to collect from the Ganjam Diftrict, out of which he is to pay to the Company, clear of all Charges, the Sum of 415,000 Rupees annually; fo that 50,000 Rupees are allowed him for his Trouble and the Charges of collecting his Revenues; a Revenue that has not been collected for the Company thefe five Years, under more than double that Expence. Ball Kiftnah alfo engages to pay the Company 40,000 Rupees a Year during his Leafe, on Account of old Balances due from the Zemindars to the Company.

He alfo further engages to pay the Company 20,000 Rupees *per Annum*, until a Lack of Rupees be paid off, that is faid to be due to the Company from Jaggabundy Chowdree's Account of the Ganjam Havelly Lands. Jaggabundy Chowdree had afferted that this Sum was due from Ball Kiftnah, but Ball Kiftnah contradicted it by the laft Letter from Ganjam: The Gentlemen there could not prove it, though no Endeavour was wanting to do it: Their own Words are " much as Ball Kiftnah may be fcreened by an artful Conduct, " and impoffible as it may be to eftablifh the Fact on pofitive Proof;" and they acknowledge that Jaggabundy Chowdree had in his Poffeffion the Accounts of Collections and Payments for 1776.

Jaggabundy Chowdree had ever been looked upon as the Renter of the Havelly Lands, recommended to the Board of Madras for his good Conduct, and could not prove that he was not the Renter, from all Circumftances put together it appears that the Sum above-mentioned was due from Jaggabundy Chowdree, and not from Ball Kiftnah; his Agreement to pay the Amount was an additional Benefit to the Company, who did not appear to ftand much chance to get it, if Ball Kiftnah had not engaged to pay it. It may not be amifs to infert the following Extracts relative to this Tranfaction.

The Governor and Council of Madras in the Year 1776, wrote to the Committee of Circuit, that Jaggabundy Chowdree, the Renter of the Havelly Lands, had been recommended to them by the Chief and Council of Ganjam, as a Man deferving of their Favour, on Account of his general good Conduct and Punctuality in performing his Engagements. (Vide Letter from Ganjam 14th January 1779.)

The

The Ganjam, Chief, and Council, say, "Jaggabundy Chowdree, has asserted to us, *(to our Astonishment)* that he had nothing to do with the Ganjam Havelly Lands.—That Ball Kistnah was the Renter: that it could be proved by all the People making the Collections."

Ball Kistnah was accordingly called on by the Governor and Council of Madras. He contradicts the Whole that Jaggabundy Chowdree had asserted, and that this Matter had been in Dispute in September 1778, before the Chief of Ganjam. Ball Kistnah asserted he was in Possession of several Settlements of Accounts between him and Jaggabundy Chowdree, shewing the Money was due from the latter, and that Jaggabundy Chowdree had declared himself to the Chief the real Renter.

Mr. Smith, in his Minute (vide Appendix No. 61,) says,—There was collected while he was Chief of Ganjam, from February 1774, to October 1777, 469,000 Rupees *per Annum*.—In the Year ending April 1778, there was collected only Rupees 342,000.—In the Year ending April 1779, there was said to be collected 500,000 Rupees: but it was only said to be, for though this last Sum was entered on the Company's Books, no such Sum was received; Information had been sent to Madras *that* the Gentlemen at Ganjam, in order to enable them to write to Madras, that their Collections for the Year ending April 1779, 500,000 Rupees, had put down in the Ganjam Accounts near 200,000 Rupees more than had been received.

This Information, and an Account of the Particulars, was sent to Ganjam, by the Governor and Council of Madras, and the Chief of that Settlement. The Cash-keeper acknowledged in Answer, that the Information was right. This great Receipt of 500,000 Rupees was only on Paper; no such Sum had been received to the 30th of April 1779:—from that Period to the End of September 1779, near Half a Year, no Revenue worth mentioning was brought to the Credit of the Company; but all that was received in that Time, which was near two Lacks or 200,000 Rupees, was carried to realize the 500,000 Rupees which was said to be collected and brought to account in the Year ending April 1779.

The Madras Confultations will fhew the Papers of Information fent to Ganjam, and the Acknowledgment received from thence of the Truth. Suppofe for Argument Sake, that the Collections for the Year ending 30th April 1779, were made as *partially* ftated from Ganjam, the Revenue of the two Years after Mr. Smith left that Chieffhip, amounted one Year with another to 422,000 Rupees a Year, during his four Years Chieffhip. He fays in his Minute, the Collections amounted to 469,000 Rupees *per Annum*; fo, for fix Years preceding the Agreement made with Ball Kiftnah, the Ganjam Collections never amounted one Year with another, to more than 455,000 Rupees *per Annum*. In order to be at a Certainty of the Benefit of the Collections to the Company, it was neceffary to fee what the Expences of making thefe Collections were, thereby to fhew how much clear Gain the Company derived from them. The Company's Books will fhew that during thefe fix Years, the Expences of Field and other military Charges of Stores, &c. the civil Charges and civil Stores for Sale, &c. fent from Madras annually, and the Affiftance of Troops from other Settlements, amounted to within 30,000 Pagodas a Year, as much as all the Revenue collected.

With regard to the Peace of the Ganjam Diftrict being fully eftablifhed, at the Time it was rented to Ball Kiftnah, as the Chief and Council, and Mr. Smith reprefented. The Madras Records will fhew, that thefe Affertions were not to be depended on, that fuch Affertions had been made over and over again. And that the Government of Madras had been given to expect every Expedition would be the laft; and yet, Expedition after Expedition ftill went on, and fwallowed up the greateft Part of the Revenue.

No. IX.

Copy of a Letter from Edward Cotsford, Efq; Chief of Mafulipatam, to the Honourable Thomas Rumbold, Governor of Fort St. George.

Dated, 6th March, 1779.

Dear Sir,

" I Send you thefe few Lines by Ball Kiftnah, the Ganjam Dubafh;
" to ferve him for an Introduction. He folicited this Favour
" with fo much Earneftnefs, that I could not refufe it, to the
" Memory

"Memory of his paſt Services. He is thoroughly acquainted with
"the Affairs of the Ganjam Country, and during my Reſidence
"there ſerved the Company, as I have every Reaſon to think, with
"Fidelity and Ability. I underſtand the Revenue of that Diſtrict
"is conſiderably reduced from what it was at the Time I left it,
"this may be owing to various Cauſes, many or ſome at leaſt
"ariſing from the Differences in the Manner of conducting Things.
"This, I confeſs, wears the Appearance of a Compliment paid to
"myſelf, but I rather chuſe to wave on this Occaſion; the con-
"ſulting a Point of Delicacy, or a ſtrict Adherence to the Rules of
"Propriety, than deny doing the Juſtice which I owe to this Man's
"Merit:—And I hope I ſhall ſtand excuſed, therefore, for ſuggeſt-
"ing that the Ganjam Collections may have ſuffered more from the
"Change of Government, and, perhaps, new Methods of conduct-
"ing Buſineſs, than from any Miſconduct or Inattention of the
"Bearer, whoſe good Behaviour under me furniſhes a ſtrong Pre-
"ſumption in his Favour. I hope you will excuſe my Freedom in
"obſerving upon this particular, having done it with no other
"View than to obviate what I apprehended might become the
"Foundation of a Prejudice againſt a Perſon I have undertaken to
"make known to you. If upon further Enquiry it ſhould appear
"that his Conduct has not been faulty, I could wiſh to ſtrengthen
"his Claim on the Score of Merit and Services, by warmly recom-
"mending him to your Protection, to which I may add, that I
"think you will find no Perſon more capable of giving you ſatis-
"factory Information, either reſpecting the Reſources, or the future
"Management of that Diſtrict, or more capable of ſerving the
"Company there.

   I am, Sir,

     Your very faithful

       And obedient Servant,

         Edward Cotsford.

No. X.

Extract of a Letter from the Chief and Council of Ganjam, to the President and Council of Fort St. George.

Dated 17th September, 1778.

" WE most solemnly declare that we have not, directly or indirectly, encouraged Ball Kistnah to disregard your Orders, but on the contrary, that we have used every Argument to induce him to comply with them, by setting off without Loss of Time.

(Signed)   Morgan Williams,
R. S. Maunsell,
T. Oakes.

No. X.

Letter from Mr. T. Oakes, of the Council at Ganjam, to Ball Kistnah.

Dated Madras, 15th May 1778.

KISTNAH,

WHEN the Rajahs and the Company's Head Dubash were ordered up to Madras, I wrote a Letter to Mr. Maunsell, giving him my Opinion, and I wonder you have not written me a Line on the Subject.

The Distance from the Ganjam District is so great that I should not be surprized if the Rajahs would say, their Country would go to Ruin in their Absence (as would in some Measure be the Case) and that they had not Money to undertake so expensive a Journey, which I believe also is very true; and should this be the Case, I imagine there would be no Occasion for you to come to Madras, because your Presence here could only be of Use in Case the Rajahs were to come down; and if they will not, or cannot come, there will be but small Collections if you leave Ganjam: Therefore, Kistnah, I would recommend it to you if the Rajahs do not leave the District to stay where you are for the Present, until further Orders.

At

At all Events I recommend it to you, to shew your Attention to Mr. Smith's Busines, and pay to Mr. Maunsell immediately on his Account the 5000 ——— you were to receive from Hautmaram, as also the Copper Money; likewise, as much of the Balance due to him as possible. Mr. Smith expects you will do all this; he wishes to be your Friend, but he must see you attend to his Affairs; he is in much Interest, and will be able to assist your Busines in every Thing.

I am a little angry that you have not written me one Line about other Matters. I shall soon return to Ganjam, where you will always, I hope, find me your Friend.

T. Oakes.

No. XI.

STATEMENT of REVENUES in the following Districts.

1st. MASULIPATAM.

Tribute from the Zemindars before my taking Charge of the Government, Ps. 529,568 : 21 annually, or	£. 211,827 : 8
Amount of Tribute settled with the Zemindars, after my taking Charge of the Government, Ps. 564,249 : 11 : 20, or - - - -	225,699 : 14
Annual Increase - -	£. 13,872 : 6
Farms under Masulipatam, lett for Ps. 5000 more than ever they before were rated for, or annual Increase - - - - - - -	2,000 : 0

2d. VIZAGAPATAM.

Amount of Tribute from the Zemindars, before my Arrival, -	Rupees 470,000	
Tribute settled in my Government	601,000	
Annual Increase -	Rs. 131,000 or	£. 14,737 : 10
Additional Revenue *per Annum* on the above Districts		£. 30,609 : 16

No. 12.

Confiderations fubmitted to Sir Thomas Rumbold by Mr. Whitehill.

UNDER the various Confiderations herein referred to, Mr. Whitehill fubmits to Sir Thomas Rumbold, whether to an Adminiftration conducted with that Firmnefs and Regularity, which have fo diftinguifhed his Government from that of moft of his Predeceffors; it may not be a proper and neceffary Appendix, to eftablifh the Succeffion to the expected Vacancies, upon fuch fecure Grounds, as may afford a Profpect of undifturbed Tranquillity during that Period, which muft be fuppofed to elapfe before the Company's Orders, in Confequence of Sir Thomas Rumbold's Departure, can be received in Europe.—A Period of fo much the more Importance from the prefent alarming State of Affairs in the Weftern Quarter of the Globe, where the Interefts of the Nation are in continual Hazard; and from the uncertain Iffue of the Negociations now fubfifting between the Supreme Council of Fort-William and the moft powerful of all the Indian States.

Let it therefore occur, though it were but for a Moment, to the candid Reflection of Sir Thomas Rumbold, whether in Times like thefe, our Councils, our judicial Proceedings, in fine, our moft fecret and important Deliberations, ought to be left expofed to the poifonous and deftructive Influence of a Man, whofe Temper and Difpofition have been marked, throughout the various Courfe of every fucceeding Government, to be of the moft turbulent and mifguided Nature.—Ever ready to watch for, and feek Opportunities of weakening the very Sinews of Government, by ftirring up Divifions amongft its Members; without any Object fo connected with the Company's Welfare, as to authorife, or even extenuate in the fmalleft Degree, a Conduct fo pregnant with Mifchief to their Affairs.—
A Man, who almoft from his firft Acceffion to a Seat in Council, gave unqueftionable Signs of this malignant Turn; and who foon after indulged it to fuch an Extent, as occafioned him to be for a while fufpended, by a Vote of Government, though Lenity induced

duced the President and Council of that Time to revoke his Suspension immediately after, he having delivered in a penitential Recantation of his contumacious Proceeding.—The Sequel of his Behaviour as a Member of the Board, the Records sufficiently shew to have been in no Shape inconsistent with this Specimen of his natural Propensity to Litigation; and to do Justice to his Ingenuity, he does not appear (as far as I can discern) to have let slip any Occasion of exercising this his favourite Principle.—Our own Experience; I mean, since the Arrival of Sir Thomas Rumbold, is strongly corroborative of the Sentiments herein conveyed respecting Mr. Johnson; and though many Circumstances of Discordance, created by Opposition on his Part to Sir Thomas Rumbold's Administration, have, from the most benevolent of Motives, been passed over in Silence, we are not the less conscious of the Existence of a Source from whence they have arisen, and from whence, in a less tranquil Season, the most dangerous Consequence may, not unjustly, be apprehended.—I would beg Leave, in Duty to the Company, to recommend the Measure; and which I am persuaded, for the Reasons herein-before set forth, will meet with your firm Concurrence and Support.

No. XIII.

Copy of a Letter from Sir Thomas Rumbold, Governor of Fort Saint George, to Mess. Matthew Raper and Charles Cromlin; Canton.

Dated Fort St George, 8th August, 1778.

Gentlemen,

BY the Royal George I sent you a Bill on Mess. Bradshaw and Pigou for 25,000 Pagodas, on Account of General Munro and myself, requesting you would remit the same to Europe.—I have only now to mention, that should it so happen, that no Remittance through the publick Companies, the English, Dutch or Swedes, is procurable, that you will please to lodge our Money in the Company's

Cash,

Cash, even without Interest, till a favourable Opportunity offers, sooner than lend it, on any Conditions, at Interest in China.

I am, Gentlemen,
Your most obedient
Humble Servant,
(Signed) Thomas Rumbold,

No. XIII.

Letter from Sir Thomas Rumbold to Matthew Raper, jun. and Charles Cromlin, Esquires, Canton.

Dated Fort Saint George, 30th July, 1779.

Gentlemen,

I Was duly favoured with your Letter of the 14th December, advising me of the Receipt of 25,000 Pagodas from Mess. Bradshaw and Pigou, and the Sale of them at 170 Spanish Dollars per 100 Pagodas, which is entirely satisfactory to Sir Hector Munro and myself, who are equally concerned in the Remittance. We have not yet received the Accounts you promised us, but have no Doubt the Money was sent home in the Company's Cash, agreeably to your Expectations.

I am, Gentlemen,
Your most obedient
Humble Servant,
(Signed) Thomas Rumbold,

No. XIV.

Copy of a Letter from Major George Maul, Chief Engineer of Fort Saint George, to Sir Thomas Rumbold, Governor.

Dated 6th April, 1780.

MY Ignorance of your Intention to embark so early this Morning, alone prevented my waiting upon you at the Beach.

As I am sure it will be equally satisfactory to yourself to receive Assurances from me, as to convey such to the Court of Directors, that the Fort will certainly in the Course of three or four Months be entirely compleated; and that the Ditch thereof, is at this Time in all its Parts cleaned out, and furnished with its intended Depth of Water. I take the Liberty of giving you this Trouble, which I the rather flatter myself you will excuse, as the Hurry of your Departure did not afford me the Honour of a Conversation with you on this Subject.

With every Wish for your perfect Recovery, and Enjoyment of all Health and Happiness, I am, dear Sir, with Respect,

Your much obliged
Devoted humble Servant,
(Signed)   George Maule.

No. XV.

Extract of a Minute of Sir Thomas Rumbold, President and Governor of Fort St. George, on resigning the Government.

AS the heavy Work of the Fortifications is now finished, and what remains of the Brick-work, we are assured by the Engineer and Contractors, will be compleated in a very short Time, this Presidency will be eased from a very great and heavy Expence; and it will depend on the Select Committee to prevent any new Works from being undertaken, without first receiving the Company's express Orders. It is with Pleasure I observe, the Nabob has punctually paid up the Engagements he entered into for the last Year, there remaining but a trifling Balance from him on Account of his February Kist.

The Rajah of Tanjore has also nearly paid up his Kist for February, on Account of his Subsidy, though no further Part of the deposit Money has been received; and in his several Letters, he has constantly pleaded his Inability to make it good. So much depends on the Punctuality of the Nabob and the Rajah of Tanjore, in the Payment of the Sums that become due from them, that I cannot too strongly recommend to my Successor, to give his utmost Attention to this particular Point; and as the Northern Revenues will now be coming in more regularly than they have for some Time past, (as our Letters from the Northern Settlement give us Reason to expect) I am in Hopes the Government will not be so much distressed with respect to the Finances, as it has been; especially if there are no Troubles in the Country, and our Troops are not obliged to take the Field. The military Operations we have been engaged in, have bore hard upon the Resources of this Presidency; which on a Peace Establishment, will do no more than answer the current Charges, and furnish the Investments.

The Maintenance of the French Prisoners, and the sending them to Europe and the Islands, has also been a great Charge, from which the Government will now be relieved, as most of them will embark in the Ships under Dispatch.

The

The Jaghire having been rented to the Nabob for three Years, of which, rather more than a Year and a half is yet unexpired, and the Nabob having wrote to me, defiring it may be granted him in a future Leafe for twenty Years, which Letter has been laid before the Board, and mentioned to the Company; it is probable, the Board will not think it neceffary to take any further Steps, relative to the Jaghire, until their Pleafure is known. I have therefore only to mention, that the Nabob has fully paid into the Treafury, the Amount of the laft Kift due from him.

No. XVI.

Tranflation of a Letter, figned and fealed by the under-mentioned Munfubdars, Jagheerders, Zemindars, &c. to the Honourable ~~Sir~~ Thomas Rumbold, ~~Baronet,~~ Prefident and Governor of Fort Saint George.

Dated 5th. Dec. 1778.

IN Confequence of the Orders we received from your Honour, to repair to Madras, in order to fettle our Tribute with the Company; and that the feveral Difputes that had happened amongft us might be enquired into; we now, in Confequence of your Permiffion, return to our own Country; and before we take our Leave and quit Madras, we return you our fincere Thanks, for your having adjufted our Difputes according to Juftice, which has afforded us great Satisfaction and Joy; and we, with all our Families, are always wifhing for an Increafe of your Honour's Health and Profperity.

Mirza Rajah Vizeram Rauze Bahauder Munna Sultan.
Mirza Rajah Seeteram Rauze Bahaudar Munna Sultan.
Rajah Opparow Bahaudar.
Rajah Jaganatha.
Rajah Triputy Rauze Bahaudar, Dufhmook of the Circars of Ellore.
Rajah Caukerlapoondy Comera.
Atchuteram Rauze, Zemindar of Cotah.

www.ingramcontent.com/pod-product-compliance
Lightning Source LLC
Chambersburg PA
CBHW021918180426
43199CB00032B/591